CONTENT-BASED NETWORKING

CONTENT-BASED NETWORKING

HOW TO INSTANTLY CONNECT WITH ANYONE YOU WANT TO KNOW

JAMES CARBARY

LIONCREST
PUBLISHING

CONTENT-BASED NETWORKING

How to Instantly Connect with Anyone You Want to Know

ISBN   978-1-5445-0397-4 *Hardcover*

978-1-5445-0396-7 *Paperback*

978-1-5445-0395-0 *Ebook*

978-1-5445-0734-7 *Audiobook*

For Jeff Flournoy

Thanks for teaching me that a single relationship can change the course of someone's entire life. This book wouldn't exist without you.

CONTENTS

INTRODUCTION

Secret: I don't read introductions. And I have a hunch a lot of other people don't read them either. So I didn't bother writing one.

You can now skip to chapter 1. :)

RELATIONSHIPS ARE EVERYTHING

CHAPTER 1

CAN WE PLAN SERENDIPITY?

I remember exactly where I was when I got the phone call. I was at a Mexican restaurant in Dallas, Texas, when my roommate called and asked me the most ridiculous question I'd ever been asked.

"James, do you want to take a private jet to New York City to watch the New York Giants play the Dallas Cowboys?"

My roommate went on to explain that his brother-in-law had just won one of those sweepstakes that you see on TV (you know, the ones we all assume nobody actually wins). The grand prize was a trip to an NFL football game of his choice for up to ten friends—including transportation to the game in a private jet, a tour of the city in a chartered limo bus, and our own catered private suite to watch the game.

"So, how about it?" he said. "Are you in?"

Well, I really had to think about it. I could stay home and watch another episode of *Lost*. Or, 10 buddies and I could fly a private jet to one of the most exciting cities in the world, where we would then be chauffeured to an NFC East rivalry game that most football fans would give up a left pinky to see.

It was a coin toss, but *Lost* had to wait.

The morning of the game, we got to the airport early and boarded our private jet. Every little detail was perfect—practically unlimited food options, fancy leather seats, and more than enough room to take an ample number of selfies. We were all acting like third graders that had just been let out for recess. Clearly, none of us had ever received the full Justin Bieber treatment before. But what was no doubt a typical Tuesday for the Biebs was brand new to us (and I'm sure it was obvious to anyone that saw us that day).

Soon, we landed. As we walked off the jet, we saw Barry Sanders—yes, *the* Barry Sanders, legendary Hall of Famer, one of the most prolific running backs in NFL history—standing there to greet us. One round of handshakes later, he told us that he'd be joining us in our private suite that evening to watch the game.

My jaw hit the floor.

Then, seemingly out of nowhere, our chartered limo bus pulled up with a police escort to tour us around New York City. In a whirlwind of activity, we took in as many sights as we possibly could—the Empire State Building, Carnegie Deli, Times Square...you name it, we saw it.

Early in the day, I noticed that we'd picked up an extra passenger for our tour of New York City: a guy named Jeff. I struck up a conversation with him and learned that he was overseeing all the transportation for our experience that day; he'd chartered the jet, rented the limo bus, and even arranged the police escort. To make sure everything went smoothly, he would be with us the entire day.

Jeff and I instantly hit it off, talking about business, faith, marriage, and everything in between. Everywhere we went—whether it was on the bus, walking through Times Square, or at the game—I kept peppering him with questions. I discovered he was actually the *CEO* of the company that had arranged our transportation, and his business did a lot more than escort wide-eyed sweepstakes winners. Jeff's company, a global logistics firm called ETA Executive Services (etaexec.com), regularly managed the transportation for major brands at events like the Super Bowl, the Grammys, and the Olympics.

The more I learned, the more fascinated I was by his story. By the time the night was over, I realized I'd spent more time chatting with Jeff than I'd spent watching the football game. On our way back to the airport later that night, we swapped email addresses.

I didn't really expect to stay in touch, so I was pleasantly surprised when he reached out to me a few months later. He called me, and we began to develop a relationship over the next several months.

About a year later, that relationship would change the trajectory of my entire life. I was sitting in my cubicle at the oil and gas company where I was working at the time. I looked down at my phone and saw that Jeff was calling. He asked me if I wanted to move to Orlando and run the helicopter division of his company. My primary job would be working with the company's NASCAR client base, helping guys like Jeff Gordon get to and from racetracks via helicopters.

I thought to myself, "What? This is a real job!?"

I prayed about it for the next few days and ultimately decided to take Jeff up on his offer. In short order, I packed up my entire life, moved halfway across the country, and settled in for the ride of a lifetime.

Three and a half years after moving to Florida, I met the

most thoughtful and caring woman on the face of the planet and was somehow able to talk her into marrying me.

As if that wasn't enough, Jeff's mentorship over those three years at his company taught me that I have what it takes to become an entrepreneur. Working for Jeff ultimately led me to start Sweet Fish Media, a podcast-first media company that produces content for a wide variety of industries.

> Eventually I began to wonder, was there a way to create life-changing relationships on-demand?

It's no exaggeration to say Jeff impacted my life in phenomenal ways—I moved across the country, was inspired to start my own business, and found the love of my life in the city I now called home, all because of my relationship with him. My once-in-a-lifetime trip to New York City turned out to be much more than a cool story, simply because I *happened* to meet Jeff.

But eventually I began to wonder, was there a way to create life-changing relationships on-demand? Was it possible to purposely engineer relationships, like the one Jeff and I had developed, to help someone get closer to their goals and dreams in life? And was it possible to put myself in a situation where I could meet another person like Jeff, without relying on a one-in-a-million circumstance?

The more I asked myself these questions, the more I realized that what happened with Jeff could happen again. And I wouldn't need to win a sweepstakes to make it happen.

CHAPTER 2

RELATIONSHIPS AREN'T THE SIDE DISH. THEY'RE THE WHOLE BUFFET

Just in case you skipped chapter 1 and my story about Jeff, here's the takeaway:

Winning an unforgettable sweepstakes put me into contact with Jeff, who turned out to be the exact person I needed in my life. And my friendship with Jeff ultimately led me to move across the country, find my future wife, and start a business.

One chance relationship with the right person changed everything.

I'm not the only one who's stumbled into a relationship like this. If you're in love, that's an easy example you can point to of a life-changing relationship. But take it a step further:

- Maybe you met your spouse or significant other at a party hosted by a mutual friend.
- Maybe you landed your dream job because you happened to know the hiring manager or someone else who worked at the company.
- Maybe your decision to go to one college over another was impacted by someone (or a group of someones) you knew at a particular school.
- Maybe you started a business, because you had the right connections.
- Maybe you happen to know the security guard at a Taylor Swift concert, so you were let in backstage.
- Maybe you know someone who works at the Happiest Place on Earth, so your niece was able to meet her favorite Disney princess...*without* waiting in a three-hour line.
- Maybe you have a family friend who works for an airline, so you've flown all around the world without paying a dime.

In each of those cases, one word jumps out: relationship.

Relationships are more than a nice side dish in life. They're the entrée, the appetizer, the side dish, and really, the whole buffet. Gary Smalley put it this way: "Life is relationships; the rest is just details."

No matter what your goals are, relationships are the rocket ship to get you there. This isn't a new idea. You can go throughout history and see how this has played out. In fact, I doubt you can point to a single historical event that wasn't based primarily on relationships.

- Caesar Augustus becoming emperor? His relationship with Julius Caesar.
- William Shakespeare's stories? Based off relationships.
- Queen Elizabeth II? She is loved and respected across the world not only because of her grace, her birthright, or her longevity, but because she spent years traveling the world building relationships with others, visiting over 100 countries.
- Not to get too romantic on you, but you are literally alive right now because two people probably formed a relationship...and then you came along.

Life starts with, ends with, and revolves around, relationships.

> Whatever you're looking to achieve, someone out there has the tools, the know-how, and the connections to help you do it.

When it comes to our careers, we've all heard "your network is your net worth." And it's true. Whatever you're looking to achieve, someone out there has the tools, the know-how, and the connections to help you do it. We can all probably agree with that. Every actor knows that Spielberg can put them in the perfect role. Every person trying to land their dream job with Google knows if they could just meet with someone high enough up the food chain, they could prove their worth and land the job.

We all agree that a relationship with the right "someone" could be our ticket to starring in the movies, our "in" with the hiring manager of our dream job, or the monetary investment we need to take our business to the next level.

The problem is that most of us don't know how to create those relationships. We chalk them up to, "Being in the right place at the right time." We sit back, wait for serendipity to run its course, and hope that great opportunities somehow fall into our laps.

We *hope* that we meet our next customer at the local chamber of commerce meeting. We *hope* that one of our LinkedIn connections can introduce us to someone with deep pockets that wants to help fund our nonprofit. We *hope* we know someone who works at the same company where we want to work, so they can move our resume to the top of the stack.

But, should we really live our lives waiting for that chance encounter to change our course?

Don't get me wrong. As the story of my meeting with Jeff illustrates, I owe *a lot* to serendipity and hope. However, *serendipity and hope aren't things we can create on-demand.* In business, we'd say that the happenstance relationship Jeff and I built isn't "scalable" (easy to replicate in the future by using the same effort that was applied in the past). These sorts of chance encounters are strokes of good luck, blessings, and serendipity. These types of strategic relationships aren't repeatable, and they're based entirely on factors outside of our control.

Serendipity and hope aren't things we can create on-demand.

Well, that's what I thought *before.*

As it turns out, pivotal relationships *are* scalable. There *is* a process we can all follow to remove chance and insert intent. You actually *can* bypass serendipity and go straight to the CEO's office, the investor's table, or the meeting with Jeff.

That's why I wrote this book.

I've found a way to take chance out of the equation. I call it Content-Based Networking.

CHAPTER 3

SO, WHAT IS CONTENT-BASED NETWORKING?

To say I was excited was an understatement.

We had just closed a business deal that often takes *months* or sometimes *years* to close. Guess how long it took us? *Less than a week.*

Here's the coolest part: We didn't land this deal by sending tons of harassing emails. We didn't even ask *one person* the stereotypical, lame question, "Hey, can I have 15 minutes of your time? We have a great product you may be interested in."

We also didn't bother doing a sales call. Not even one.

But still, we managed to get not just 15 minutes, but close to an hour with the *exact* person we needed to connect with.

We didn't sell them anything. We talked to them. And then, less than a week later, they signed a six-month contract for one of our services, a podcast production service specifically for B2B (business-to-business) companies.

(Now, if you're not in B2B sales, this may sound pretty boring—*Who cares about a B2B podcasting service?*—But landing a six-month contract in less than a week is sort of like getting cast in a speaking role for a movie on your first try. So just picture that scenario, and you'll have an idea of how unusual this was.)

Needless to say, my whole team and I were ecstatic that we had such "luck."

But it actually wasn't luck at all.

We intentionally put ourselves in the right place, at the right time, with the right person.

Here's how the six-day deal happened:

(Side note before we jump into this: Even if you aren't in "sales," everyone needs to connect with the *right* person.

Whether you're an entrepreneur that wants meetings with potential customers, an aspiring actor trying to meet casting directors, or a recent college graduate trying to connect with hiring managers, this process is pretty much the same.)

To start, we figured out *who* we needed to connect with. We knew what product we were trying to sell and who ultimately had the authority to purchase this product.

We knew that we needed to connect with VPs of Marketing at B2B technology companies with 50-plus employees.

So, through our research, we found someone, we'll call her Marie, who—guess what—is a VP of Marketing at a B2B technology company with 50-plus employees (we'll call the company Acme Corp—original, I know).

We then sent her an email, bombarding her with questions and telling her how great our product is.

Actually, no. That's not what we did. Because that doesn't work.

Here's what we *actually* did. We sent her an email that said something like this:

Hey Marie—saw that Acme was featured in *Forbes* recently,

and I'd love to feature you on our podcast (*B2B Growth*). Up for it?

Yes, that's how long the email was.

Guess what?

Marie said yes.

So, she came on our show, and we had a great time chatting as we recorded the content for our episode. Marie talked about her experience, the lessons she'd learned, why certain strategies worked, and why others had failed.

After 20 minutes, we finished recording the episode. We kept chatting off-line, and I learned something that I did *not* know about Marie and her company.

It turns out that Marie's company was looking to invest in their CEO's thought leadership. They had been discussing starting their own podcast but just didn't have the bandwidth within their organization to pull it off.

Here's what I told her:

> We actually offer a done-for-you podcasting service and we specifically work with B2B tech companies, just like yours.

She wasn't mad. She didn't hang up on me. She didn't say, "Well, this was a sham." She didn't even try to let me down easy by saying, "We'll think about it." She just said. "Wow. That sounds awesome."

And, six days later, she signed up to work with us.

So, yes, we were in the right place at the right time.

But if you noticed, being in the right place, at the right time, and with the right person, was *intentional.*

We didn't know that Marie and her team had just been discussing starting a podcast. But we *did* know we were the exact right service for her company, and that she was exactly the person we needed to connect with. So we engineered a meeting with her *on purpose.* We didn't just *hope* we ended up with someone like Marie, we mindfully went after the relationship with her, and we did it in a way that we knew would work. And, here's the deal, we do it *all the time*, and we've helped lots and lots of other people put themselves in the room with *their* Marie as well.

So, how did we do it?

We used Content-Based Networking to reverse-engineer the entire scenario.

If you're thinking, "Wait, isn't reverse-engineering what people who steal patents do?" Well, yes, yes it is. But, reverse-engineering is also what you do every time you pack for a vacation. You think, "OK, Tuesday, I'm going to the beach. If I'm at the beach, I'll need a swimsuit. Wednesday, we're going to that fancy French place. For that, I'll need a nice outfit." When you're packing for a vacation, you start at the end, and you work your way backwards. And here's why we pack that way:

> The end is a great place to start.

When you start at the end, you aren't guessing. You know exactly where you want to go (or, in the case of traveling, how you want to look when you arrive). And in fact, the end is where you start every good strategy. You tell yourself, "This end goal is what I want. Now, how do I build every step from there, back to my starting place?"

And that's exactly what Content-Based Networking is. It's starting from the end, from the relationship you want to build, and working *back* to the starting line.

People all over the world want to get to know casting directors, hiring managers at companies they want to work for, or people like Marie who can buy their product. But the problem is, they usually fall short of connecting with those people. They have a clear picture of what they want, but they don't have a clear picture on how to get there. So, they start and they hope...and too often, don't make it very far. They never make it to the casting director, the hiring manager, or the business partnership. Or, maybe they *do* finally get the email address for that hiring manager, but when they send out a cold email, it falls flat because it's awkward.

I get it.

We all need relationships, but creating them on-demand is nearly impossible without a framework.

Here's what we are going to do in this book: We are going to give you a framework, called Content-Based Networking, to work *backwards* from the exact goals you have in mind, from the place you want to *end up*, the connections that you need, and the relationships that will help you achieve your goals and dreams.

To meet with Marie, I worked my way backwards from the goal I had. I didn't just *hope* we would cross paths, I engineered the path-crossing. And, I didn't just *hope* I had something valuable for Marie, I was sure of it.

And, over the last few years, it's been a wild ride helping scores of others do the same thing I did: meet the exact people who could help them reach their goals. I've seen companies start, speaking gigs get landed, businesses flourish, friendships accelerate, and the list goes on and on. I can't wait to see how you use Content-Based Networking to put yourself in the room with *your* Maries.

But just before we dive into the concept of strategically building relationships, I'm going to give you a few spoilers up front, just so we're on the same page as we get rolling.

1. Content-Based Networking takes work. It isn't a "become a millionaire while you sleep" sort of methodology.
2. I own a podcast-first media company that works specifically with B2B (business-to-business) companies, so many of my examples come from that world. But don't worry. I'll also talk about sports, acting, art, Taylor Swift, and plenty of other non-businessy examples as well.
3. I believe relationships are about far more than just monetary or career results. So, if you're simply trying to hack your way into someone's office or burst into someone's pocketbook without really caring about them, then this book isn't for you. Content-Based Networking only works if you care about the people you're building relationships with, regardless of whether or not you get anything in return.

Cool. Glad we got that out of the way. Let's get rolling.

> Relationships are about far more than just monetary or career results.

CONTENT-BASED NETWORKING EXPLAINED

Content-Based Networking is networking based on...wait for it...CONTENT. It's figuring out, like I did with Marie, who you need to connect with (what we'll call *goals*), then reaching out to them (which we talk about in the *people* section), and then collaboration (*creating content with the people you want to know*—this is the important part).

A lot of people can handle the first two on their own (the *goals* and the *people*), but they miss the third (and crucial) piece of the equation—the *content*.

They start out with figuring out who their Maries are, and then they reach out to them. Guess what usually happens? Their Maries never respond with an "I would love to meet with you too—I'm in!" In fact, they don't even bother responding at all. Sometimes, if you push too hard, Marie gets annoyed, you end up damaging your reputation, and ultimately you ruin future opportunities.

People start with their *goals*—the connections they are trying to build—then they move to what I call the *people* phase, and then they stop. But here's the magic piece: *content*. The content collaboration with Marie was the crucial piece in getting the opportunity to do business with her—content is the *reason* she met with me. Content is the difference between sending out a random message to a complete stranger (which is what most people do) and sending out a warm invite to a soon-to-be friend (which is what Content-Based Networking shows you how to do).

The content is the difference between selflessly asking the other person for something they can do for you and offering something for *them*. When I asked Marie to be on our *show*, I talked about what *I had to offer her.* I gave her a chance to share her story, and to talk about herself. Instead of asking Marie for something, I offered her a chance to promote herself and the company she works for, something very few people say *no* to. I simply created an opportunity, around our show, for her to be featured as a guest. Then, we talked. Through the course of the conversation (the podcast interview), we got to know each other. I found out about her challenges, her *goals*, and her story. Within just a few minutes, we were more than mere acquaintances. We had built a relationship that simply *could never* have flourished if I had simply said, "Hey Marie, we're a podcast-first media company. Would you like to hear about our services?"

So, to answer the question, "What is Content-Based Networking?"

Content-Based Networking is using content collaboration to build the exact relationships that can help you achieve your *goals* and dreams. Content-Based Networking is figuring out the relationships you need to build to achieve your *goals*, going directly to those people, and creating content with them.

Imagine you're on the ground floor and your *goals* are up on the top floor of a skyscraper. The only problem? There's no elevator—and no stairs. You could rely on hope and serendipity. You could wait for a helicopter to come along and offer you a ride. You could pray for some rock climbers to show up and offer you a free piggyback ride to the top.

But instead, you decide to take the whole situation into your own hands.

You reverse-engineer the scenario. You ask yourself, "To arrive at the top floor, my end goal, what connection do I need to make between the top and the bottom?" You determine what materials you'll need, what plan to follow, and what tools to use to build your own staircase. That's Content-Based Networking—getting yourself to the top floor *on purpose*. That staircase you're going to build? That's your network. And the individual blocks, the steps that make up the set of stairs? Those are pieces of content you are going to create.

I know that's a pretty theoretical analogy; I just used that staircase example because I was told analogies are super helpful to some people.

But I'm a literal, action sort of guy.

To show how this staircase would work in real life, here are a couple examples:

- Jamie is a musician that wants to be signed to a record label. So she collaborates with music producers by filming them in their day-to-day work (audio engineering, scouting talent, developing songs with artists, etc.). Then she edits the footage and posts the videos to her YouTube channel.
- Kamal wants to be a chef, so he collaborates with top-rated chefs to create content about their food. He snaps pictures of the chefs in the kitchen and of their final dishes. He then publishes all of the content on Instagram, tagging all the chefs and highlighting their recipes.
- Emily wants to sell marketing software to the airline industry, so she starts a podcast that features interviews with marketing managers at different airlines. During the interviews, Emily asks the marketing managers about their career journey, the challenges of being an airline marketer, and the marketing tactics they've tested in the last six months.

In all three cases, someone had a dream they wanted to accomplish. To achieve that, they figured out who they needed to know (their *goal*). Then, they built a relationship with those *people* through collaborating on *content*. And that content is not only valuable for Jamie, Kamal, and Emily—it's also valuable for the people they're collaborating with. And, as a bonus, that content is valuable to anyone who consumes it.

That's a triple threat.

Every time Jamie, Kamal, or Emily produces a piece of content with the right people, they are building a relationship that puts them one step closer to their dreams. And, their guests are receiving tremendous value as well. The guest gets to be highlighted in that content, allowing them to grow their reach and influence. Then, for anyone *else* who is reading, watching, or listening to that content, they get value out of it too. Everyone wins.

> Content-Based Networking is valuable to everyone involved—the producer, the guest, and anyone who consumes it. It's a triple threat.

By the end of this book, you'll have a relationship-driven path to accomplishing your *goals* and dreams. You'll have a three-part framework that is repeatable, scalable, and easily usable. You will be able to take your dreams, narrow down your *goals* to the *people* you need to connect with, and, unlike the person who sends out random emails, people will meet with *you* because you'll be providing them value through the *content* you create with them. So, here's a quick preview of what we'll be covering:

1. **The *goals*.** We'll start at the beginning by defining your goals. I know what you're thinking: "I already know my goals and dreams." You probably do. We're just going to tweak them a little bit for clarity. Instead of having a goal like "Become a politician," you'll learn how to drill down to a goal like "Connect with swing voters" instead.

2. **The *people*.** Next, we're going to show you how to build those connections. Here, you'll see how to make an offer someone can't refuse and how to shine a spotlight on the work and value of others.

3. **The *content*.** The easiest way to create a genuine relationship with someone is to collaborate with them—in this case, by working together to create a piece of content. Collaborating on content also makes your content more focused, more insightful, and more effective. The content could be anything—a series of photographs, blog posts, podcasts, videos, virtual summits, industry reports, documentaries, music, you name it. With Content-Based Networking, all types of collaborative content can be the launching point of a genuine and meaningful relationship.

So that's the preview. Hopefully, it's exactly what you were hoping for, because, my guess is, you're reading this book because you want something more. You have big dreams, and you have the passion and energy to pursue them. Maybe you're an aspiring entrepreneur like I was. Maybe you're a musician hoping to serenade the world. Maybe you're an insurance agent looking to become the best provider in your city. Maybe you're a public speaker with a powerful message the world needs to hear. Whatever the case, you're not OK with sitting around, hoping that a life-changing relationship falls into your lap. You're ready to take a proactive approach to your life's narrative.

If that's you, then let's roll.

GOALS

CHAPTER 4

DON'T DRIVE TO THE WRONG COFFEE SHOP

There are only three high-level aspects of Content-Based Networking: *goals, people,* and *content.* The *goals* section is a pretty short read, but this section is crucial to ensuring you start off in the right direction. Why? Well, because of how many times you've probably ended up at the wrong place. Think about meeting your friends for coffee. If they say, "Let's meet at Starbucks," it takes about two seconds to double-check if it's the *downtown* Starbucks or the *uptown* Starbucks. Those of us who've gone to the wrong location and waited for half an hour for our friends know how important that two-second question can be.

Let's take those two seconds right here and just make sure we are plugging in the right location into our Goals

Positioning System. (See what I did there? G-P-S. Was that way too cheesy? Sorry.)

Here's what we think our *goals* are—we tend to confuse them with our high-level *dreams*. We *dream* of owning our own company, and we make that our goal. But that's not exactly what we're looking for in Content-Based Networking. The important thing here is to narrow your *goal* as specifically as possible. You want to take that wild idea about becoming a politician, starting your business, or landing your dream job and tame it into something slightly narrower that becomes a more tangible idea you can focus on. Namely, and in this context, *goal will refer to the specific relationships you are trying to create*. Basically, we're going to boil your high-level dream down to a relationship you need to build.

Sound good? OK. Great. Here's how to narrow down your dream to a goal.

Let's say your dream is: "Become a politician," "Start my business," or, "Be a world-renowned chef." We would start to peel off one layer to arrive at something like: "Become the state representative for Colorado," "Start a B2B software company," or, "Land a job as a sous chef at a high-end restaurant." Perfect. You're literally halfway there. But we want to take it further. We want to keep drilling down to a *relationship*. This concept is a little easier to illustrate with examples than it is with a bunch of theory, so I'm going to give you three examples of how people might find their *goals*.

> To make your goal more tangible, keep drilling down until you've identified the specific relationships you need to create.

AMY, THE POLITICAL HOPEFUL

Let's start with the politician who wants to be a state representative for Colorado. We'll call her Amy. Amy has dreams of reforming education, improving the economy, and serving the homeless.

To become a state representative, she needs votes, and she needs them from people within her district. Amy already has 45% of the votes, because that segment typically votes for Amy's party. What she really needs is to get votes from undecided voters, those who don't normally vote, or from new voters in her district. So, Amy does some research.

She finds that a good amount of the urbanites in her area have recently moved into town, and no one knows how they vote yet. This provides a great segment of possible new voters.

After pounding the pavement, Amy discovers that these

new urbanites are hanging out at cool mom-and-pop food joints. You know the ones we're talking about—avocado toast, slow-drip coffee, and acai bowls.

That's where she finds her new, hyper-focused goal:

Connecting with new urbanites at local mom-and-pop shops.

See? It wasn't rocket science, it didn't take too long, and now Amy has a concrete new goal.

Here are two more examples of the same process, but with different industries:

JEREMY, ASPIRING SOCK ENTREPRENEUR

Jeremy's goal is to quit his day job and go full time with his clothing company. Specifically, Jeremy makes comfortable, hilarious socks based on popular memes (OK, maybe this is a little over the top, but this is a fictional story, so go with me for a minute).

Here's what Jeremy has going for him: His socks are phenomenal, and everyone who's worn them says they're incredibly comfortable—and, of course, super funny.

Here are his liabilities: Jeremy has no retail space of his own, and his online orders are only so-so.

With his assets and liabilities in mind, Jeremy believes his best course of action is to sell his socks at retail outlets who have national distribution and multiple locations, like Macy's. But how on Earth do you actually get your clothing product into Macy's? Well, Jeremy does his research. After asking around, he discovers that he'll need to get the sign-off from the people with enough authority to make vendor-related purchasing decisions. These people have a variety of titles, usually along the lines of "buyers," "purchasing managers," "procurement managers," etc.

Taking that into account, Jeremy now has a new, narrower, and hyper-focused *goal*:

Connect with purchasing managers at chain retailers.

KAMAL, FUTURE THREE-STAR MICHELIN CHEF

Kamal's a chef. Well, not professionally (only his girlfriend and his family know how talented he is), but he's essentially Michael Phelps in the kitchen. Currently, Kamal's a junior in college, and he's getting ready to graduate with a degree in culinary arts.

Kamal is applying for internships as a sous chef...just like everyone else in his culinary arts program. He also has an incredible GPA...just like everyone else. He can even tell you that his family believes he's the world's next Gordon Ramsay...just like everyone else. (See a trend?)

But Kamal doesn't *think* like everyone else. Instead, this thought floats across his mind: "There must be a better way than just crossing my fingers and hoping someone chooses my resume out of this huge pile."

Kamal looks around and notices that the few lucky people who actually *did* get interviews for the best sous chef positions all had something in common: they somehow had connections with the head chef at the restaurant where they interviewed. He realizes that what he ultimately needs are a few head chefs to know him, like him, and trust him.

So, while his dream is "Become a three-star Michelin chef," he has a new *goal*, that he drilled down to, as specifically as possible. His new *goal* is:

Create relationships with head chefs at top-tier restaurants.

* * *

That's three examples of three different individuals all looking to fulfill different dreams. But the process to drill down to their as-specific-as-possible *goal* was the same. They started with the high-level view, then peeled off a layer or two, then did some research, then peeled off another layer, and they kept going until they understood the specific relationships they needed to develop to achieve their *goals*.

PRO TIP

If you're struggling to identify the right relationship, try this: think about somebody else who has achieved what you want to achieve. Then, ask them. No seriously. Just reach out and see if they're willing to answer a few questions about the relationships that catapulted them to success.

If you're feeling a little shy, you can always just research the person and reverse engineer their relationships until you have an idea of the secret formula that led them to the top. But I suggest reaching out. Not only will you get better answers that way, but you'll also (gasp!) *build a relationship with the exact kind of person you want to know* in the process.

THE POSSIBILITIES ARE ENDLESS

Maybe you aren't interested in being a politician, a fashionista, or a chef. No sweat. In reality, this process can be adapted to just about any context you can think of:

- To get a job, you may need to connect with hiring managers at companies where you want to work.
- To land speaking gigs, you could connect with event organizers.

- To make an impact in your local community, you could connect with city officials.
- To succeed in B2B sales, you could connect with decision-makers at your target accounts.
- To fund your start-up, you could connect with investors.
- To start or continue a nonprofit, you could connect with generous and purpose-driven individuals.
- To expand your financial planning business, you could connect with successful entrepreneurs in your city.
- To advance your career as a filmmaker, you could connect with other filmmakers and producers.
- To become an athletic coach, you could connect with professional and collegiate coaches.
- To gain visibility as an actor, you could connect with casting directors.
- To sell books as a children's author, you could connect with principals and teachers at elementary schools.
- To advance your career, you could connect with senior executives in the industry you love.

I could go on, but I think you get the picture.

Here's the big idea with *goals:* Be specific, and narrow them down as much as possible so you know exactly who you need to connect with as we roll into the next section.

Now, after considering your *goals*, you may be thinking:

"Well, I know why I would want to meet with my ideal connections and why I would want to build a relationship with them, but I have no idea why those people would want to meet with me."

That's a great thought. In fact, there is a very good reason people will want to meet with you.

Because, after you read the next chapter, you're going to be just like Oprah—and everyone wants to meet Oprah.

CHAPTER 5

BE LIKE OPRAH

You may already know Oprah's story, but in case you don't, here's the quick version: Before she became one of the world's wealthiest and most well-known celebrities, Oprah Winfrey faced tremendous adversity. Born in the small, rural town of Kosciusko, Mississippi, Oprah was tragically abused as a young child. Eventually, she ran away from home at age 14 and settled in Nashville to live with her father.

Here, her life finally began to look up. Her father's structured environment nurtured Oprah's creative side, and she soon flourished, winning prizes for oratory and dramatic recitation. But her story kept getting better. At 17, Oprah won the Miss Black Tennessee beauty pageant and was soon offered an on-air job at Nashville radio station WVOL. Later, at just 22 years old, she moved to Baltimore to join WJZ TV as a coanchor and soon co-hosted the *People Are Talking* show. Eight years later, a Chicago TV station recruited Oprah to host her own show, *AM Chicago*, which was renamed *The Oprah Winfrey Show* in 1985. A year later, the show was broadcast nationally and quickly became the number one talk show in syndication.

Every person alive wants to be on Oprah's show. Why? Because she's inspirational, she's fun, she's energetic, and she *always shines the spotlight on the other person*.

Oprah doesn't soak up credit. She isn't in this for her, and she never has a self-centered attitude. Oprah has one drive: give back to others. She does this by inviting people on her show, making them look smart and funny, and giving them a chance to share their story. Then, she takes that story and shares it with the world for others to see and be inspired.

Do you see what she's doing that's so amazing? She's not only shining a spotlight on someone else so they can have the limelight, but she's also inviting *her audience* along for the journey so they can get a peek. It's the triple threat we talked about earlier—a win-win-win. Oprah has a valuable relationship with someone, her guest. That guest gets tremendous value from being on Oprah's show. Other than just getting the chance to talk to Oprah (which, let's be real, that's amazing!), each guest now has a chance to share their dreams and passions with the world, so that's hugely valuable for them. And, the audience is brought into all the action, and is able to learn from the triumphs, mistakes, and stories of others.

That's why you want to be like Oprah—because she's a genius. She always shines a light on the guest she's bringing into center stage, and everyone watches. If you wanted a how-to on becoming an influential leader in any industry, you can't do any better than Oprah.

Plus, this answers the question you were thinking after reading the last chapter: "Why would anyone want to connect with me?" People will want to connect with you if you're like Oprah—if you're shining the light on *them*, their dreams, and their passions. That's the massive benefit you are going to offer others.

Oprah has done this with a broadcast TV show. You are going to do it with Content-Based Networking. You're going to create content somewhat similar to Oprah's, but with a much narrower focus. You'll invite people on *your* show and then shine the spotlight on them, which will help you build a genuine relationship with them.

> People will want to connect with you if you're like Oprah—if you're shining the light on them, their dreams, and their passions.

Are you starting to see it yet?

Everyone wants to meet with Oprah, because she gives them a chance to share their story. So you are going to do the exact same thing. You are going to give others a chance to share their stories, on a podcast, on a vlog, on a blog, or with photography, documentary, music...whatever you want to collaborate with others on. Oprah used a stage with video cameras. But instead, you can use a blog and ask other people questions. Or, you can have a podcast and invite people on your show. Or, you could do a series of photos focused on someone's work. It's all the same basic idea—highlighting someone else in such a way that allows both of you to work together.

That's the beauty of Content-Based Networking.

PRO TIP

Seriously, be like Oprah. You don't have to give away a room full of cars or anything (although as we'll see in chapter 13, gift-giving is a fantastic way to grow relationships). Just be interested in the people you talk to and give them a chance to tell their story.

* * *

Let's put it all together to make sure we're all set before we move on to Step 2: *People*.

You started out with your *dreams*, which is probably how you ended up with this book.

Then, you narrowed down those dreams into specific relationships you need to build. Those relationships are your new focus, and we're calling those *goals*.

Then, we answered the question, "Why will someone else want to build a relationship with me?" People will want to build a relationship with you because you are going to provide them *value,* and you're going to be like Oprah, and shine a spotlight on them, not on yourself.

One quick thing before we get going: As we move forward, we are going to use the term *guest* pretty often, and I just want to make sure that term makes sense to you. We are going to use the word *guests* to refer to the people you are trying to build relationships with. Why? Well, for one, that's what Oprah calls the people who come on her show. And we've already established the fact that we should be like Oprah. But, the other reason for using the word *guests* is that's what we'll be talking about from here on out: inviting people to collaborate on content with you

(you know, the whole Content-Based Networking thing). And when people are collaborating on content with you, we like to call them *guests*.

YOU'RE ALREADY DONE WITH AN ENTIRE SECTION OF THIS BOOK!

I think you owe yourself a big ol' glass of Cherry Coke Zero and some Red Vines licorice (the best combo of all time). Chapter 6 will be waiting for you when you're back from the kitchen!

PEOPLE

CHAPTER 6

THE SPOTLIGHT EFFECT

Now you know exactly who you want to connect with to achieve your *goals*, which is the first step in the three-part Content-Based Networking framework. We talked about why people will want to build that connection with you—because you are going to give them something. And that something is called a spotlight.

So, Step 1 was *goals* (defining the connections and relationships you are going to build).

Now, we're on Step 2: *People*. This is where you'll learn how to actually build those connections.

We talked about why you should be like Oprah and shine a spotlight on someone else. But you probably have some questions at this point, like:

- Where do I start?
- How do I get people on my show?
- Will people actually want to talk with me?

I get it.

But that brings me to the main point of this chapter: Just start. Once you have an idea, even before you have a single piece of *content*, you can rightfully say, "I have a spotlight to offer."

Once you have a spotlight to offer, you are like Oprah; you have something of value to offer the other person. Because of that, people will want to meet with you. So, if you want to start interviewing casting directors for a blog, (1) simply say you have a blog that features casting directors, and then (2) start interviewing casting directors for your brand-new blog. The same is true for any industry, and just about every medium. To start, you start. It's that simple.

I know it sounds like I'm cheating by not giving you anything solid here. So let me give you a story to show you what I mean.

> Once you have an idea, even before you have a single piece of *content*, you can rightfully say, "I have a spotlight to offer."

BE LIKE PATRICK

My friend Patrick Hodgdon is a chief storyteller. (And no, I'm not exaggerating. That's literally his title at the company he started, Story Sprints.) But before he owned his own business, Patrick was the Director of Marketing for Riptide Software. Patrick was brilliant in this role because he knew the secret behind Content-Based Networking: grab a spotlight and start shining it.

Here's how it went down.

In 2016, when Patrick came on board at Riptide, they were trying to sell a new product in the enterprise learning and development space.

Patrick's first question was, "Who's the senior-level decision-maker for our product?"

It turns out that most larger companies have a head of learning and development called a CLO (Chief Learning Officer). To engage and build relationships with CLOs, Patrick decided to start a podcast.

Here was Patrick's Content-Based Networking thought process:

> **Goal:** Connect with people that could potentially buy his company's software.

> **People:** CLOs.

> **Content:** A podcast featuring interviews with CLOs.

In case you're wondering what a CLO *does,* I couldn't tell you. And to be perfectly honest, I'm not sure that Patrick could have told you what they did either—at least not before he started the podcast. But this lack of industry knowledge didn't keep Patrick from creating *content* for this audience. So how was Patrick going to do a podcast about Chief Learning Officers without having any expertise himself? Well, guess who *does* know a lot about CLOs?

CLOs.

Patrick's next move was to attend a CLO conference the following month. At the conference, he made a point to personally thank each of the speakers, from the keynote speakers to the speakers of every single breakout session he attended. He thanked them, let them know he'd learned a lot from their talk, and told them he was brand-new to the space.

Then, he asked if he could interview them for a podcast he was going to start. Not surprisingly, he had plenty of CLOs say, "Sure! I'd love to be featured on your show!"

As a result, with no prior network in the learning and development space, and purely through Content-Based Networking, Patrick was able to interview CLOs and other heads of learning from a slew of Fortune 500 companies and other popular brands, including Sears, General Mills, The Home Depot, McKinsey & Company, GE, Xerox, the NBA, Qualcomm, and others.

I could go on and on about how successful Patrick's Content-Based Networking strategy was, but this quote from one of his podcast guests sums it up:

> I've got to hand it to you, Patrick—what you've already been able to do in just six months with this podcast, I've seen teams of 10-plus marketers try to do in 10 years and not get as far.

But here's what I love most about Patrick's story: Patrick didn't wait for a stamp of approval from the Podcast Approval Authorities (those authorities don't exist, by the way). In fact, Patrick started by just going to conferences and trade shows where CLOs hangout, and saying, "Hey, I'm creating content for CLOs, and I'd love to hear your thoughts. Care to share them?"

Boom.

Patrick had a spotlight. He didn't wait for someone to give it to him. He just grabbed it.

And he shined that spotlight on the exact people he wanted to connect with.

GRAB A SPOTLIGHT

It's pretty simple. To have a spotlight, you grab a spotlight. A hundred years ago, that may have required a lot of technical expertise, thousands of dollars, and maybe even having the same last name as someone who owned a media company.

But thanks to the internet and other modern-day technology, everyone can grab a spotlight, and the upside is that now everyone can build a community around even the most niche topics. Here's what I mean: When TV, radio, movies, etc. were incredibly expensive, only certain topics made it into the media. Now, there's a blog, a video series, a podcast, a slideshow, and a niche marketplace for literally everything. So, whatever you're super interested in doing, you can create a space for that, invite others who are interested in that same niche, and build a community around that topic. You can literally go online right now and start a blog for free. You can leverage free sites like YouTube to create a video series. There's even a lot of free tools that help you create logos. But, in all honesty, not everyone even needs an entire website or a logo.

Remember Jeremy, the aspiring entrepreneur with the awesome meme socks and the retail sales problem? We talked about him earlier in chapter 4. We helped him define his *goals*, which got him to this point:

> **Jeremy's goal:** Connect with purchasing managers at chain retailers.

So, if we were taking Jeremy through this process, now we'd walk him through the *people* phase, and get his hands on a spotlight, so he could provide his future guests—purchasing managers at chain retailers—with value.

Let's say Jeremy decided to do a blog series. He already has a website for his socks, because he sells a few online, so he just adds a spot on his website for his blog posts.

Now when he emails Sally, the purchasing manager at the Big-Name Chain Store, he's going to say something like this:

> Hey Sally, I'm writing a blog series on retail analytics, and I saw the article you wrote on LinkedIn about the topic. I thought you'd be a great person to highlight in the series. Any interest in doing a 15-minute interview?

Just like that, Jeremy has a spotlight.

SHINE THE SPOTLIGHT

Shining a spotlight is pretty simple. If you've ever worked as a lighting tech in a theater, you get the idea: *follow the person on stage.*

That's exactly what you do here. That starts with the email, with any follow-up, and with the actual interview process. The spotlight stays on the person you're connecting with. Your goal is to make them sound awesome—plain and simple. Notice how the email I just shared highlighted the person receiving the email?

You may have noticed from our email examples that we believe in research. When you're shining your spotlight on someone else, it helps to know about them in a few different areas.

> Shining a spotlight is pretty simple. Just follow the person on stage.

RESEARCH AN INDIVIDUAL (AND ANY OF THEIR CURRENT CONTENT)

I don't just believe in social media stalking.

I *really* believe in social media stalking.

No, we're not talking about being creepy and finding out anything people don't want you to know about them. I'm talking about the exact opposite—finding out everything about someone that they *do* want you to know.

Find out what they're interested in, the content they consume, awards they've won, conferences they spoke at or attended, promotions they've received, etc. Here's the deal: People use social media specifically because they *do* want people to know about certain parts of their life, especially their professional accomplishments, which is what you should be focused on. Social media platforms change pretty rapidly—at the time this book is being published, LinkedIn is a great place to find out about someone's professional life. In 2025, it may be a different social network, but the idea is the same: Use public information about someone's professional career to determine what they are passionate about.

PRO TIP

If someone has recently released content (maybe they wrote a book, spoke at a conference, were featured on a podcast, were mentioned in a news article, etc.), then that's a huge sign that they have a message to spread and they're open to press. Also, it gives you something to mention in your outreach.

RESEARCH THEIR INDUSTRY

If you're an actor trying to land a role, you probably know a lot about the industry from your perspective. What you may have overlooked, or are just not aware of, is how the industry plays out for casting directors. This goes back to that spotlight. The goal is the people you're trying to connect with, and you want to use your spotlight to follow them in their world, not you in yours. And their world as a hiring manager, casting director, investor, buyer, etc., probably looks a lot different than yours. They probably have different problems and are trying to solve different issues.

FIND WHERE YOUR FUTURE FRIENDS LIKE TO HANG OUT

Everyone has a favorite hangout. That could be a local coffee shop, a particular social media platform, a conference...you get the idea. We've found that, depending on the industry, this can really differ, but the commonality is this: people with similar experience within the same industry usually have a favorite hangout.

Here at Sweet Fish, we focus particularly on the online space, and still the hangouts are very different. If your people are hanging out on LinkedIn, you need to be there. If they're really active on Twitter, that's your in. If there's a particular event they all go to every year, get a ticket.

Once you've done your research, you'll be in a wildly better place to approach people with a spotlight.

Now, if you're thinking, "No one is going to want to talk to me, even with that spotlight," you're wrong. They will definitely talk to you. And you're about to learn the seven-part recipe that will help you make that happen.

CHAPTER 7

MASTER THE ART OF COLD EMAILS

I hate getting unsolicited emails.

OK, I hate getting *most* unsolicited emails.

You know the kind I'm talking about—I'd bet you get more than a couple yourself. You can always tell a cold, unsolicited email from a mile away. They're impersonal, oddly worded, and out of touch with reality. Many sound like they were written by a robot.

Also, I almost never want what the robot, or person, or alien, is selling me. The sender is adding no value to my life. All they want is my money.

It's no surprise, then, that the average reply rate for cold emails is absurdly low. Some say it's less than 1%. However, that's not the case with Content-Based Networking. My very first Content-Based Networking attempt, I was able to get an 80% response rate. There's a sad, simple reason why these numbers are so wildly different: Most of us suck at cold outreach. Here's the good news: You're going to learn how to craft a cold email that *doesn't* suck.

So let me put aside some fears right now—you're not trying to sell anything with Content-Based Networking. You're trying to connect and offer a spotlight.

Cold outreach (outreach to someone you've never met before) in the Content-Based Networking model is effective for a very simple reason: exposure is valuable to most people. Since you, the content creator, are now able to offer exposure in the form of your show, you have tangible value to offer someone, not just an offer to "pick their brain over coffee" or "sign up for a 15-minute software demo." Your spotlight makes you the media, and, as a media entity, you have the ability to act as a third-party endorsing someone's credibility and expertise. The person you're emailing could write an article about themselves saying how great they are, and nobody would care. However, when a third party writes an article sharing that same person's accolades and accomplishments, it means something.

> You're not trying to sell anything with Content-Based Networking. You're trying to connect and offer a spotlight.

That being said, just because you're able to shine a spotlight and offer something valuable like media exposure, doesn't mean you have a pass to sound like a grizzly coming out of hibernation. At the end of the day, you're still a complete stranger to the people you're contacting. You'll need to be thoughtful and intentional about how you initially contact these people, but when done correctly, it works.

THE 7 MUST-DOS OF GOOD OUTREACH

There are plenty of good ideas on how to get a response from people you contact. However, these seven things are a *must* in today's spammy world. Make sure you can check the following seven boxes with every single first-time message you send to someone.

1. KEEP IT SIMPLE

Too many people make the mistake of telling their whole life story in their initial outreach. They share everything in an attempt to anticipate all the recipient's possible questions. Don't ramble on about stuff that doesn't matter. Unless your name is Bill Gates, chances are the recipient of your message (who doesn't know you) doesn't care that you started your company with your buddy in your garage, and now you have 40,000 Twitter followers. Well, they don't care *yet*. Once they know you, like you, and trust you, you can share more of your story.

For now, pick one or two quick facts that make it clear that you're adding value to them.

> Hey Paul, we're doing a series of videos about your industry, and we'd love to feature you. Any interest?

See how nice and simple that is? Elaborate emails only clutter the process. They take time to create, and they take time to read. Share just enough information that confirms your credibility. If you've had 30,000 downloads of your *content* last month, say that. If your brand isn't that recognizable yet, leverage the credibility of others you've worked with. We do this with one of our podcasts, *B2B Growth*, by mentioning that Gary Vaynerchuk (or GaryVee, as many people know him) and Simon Sinek are former guests.

PRO TIP

Here's a good rule of thumb to make sure you're not going overboard: cap your emails at four sentences. Anything more, and you've probably said too much. Often, people make the mistake of thinking a long bio builds credibility, when, in fact, the opposite is true: the more you ramble on, the quicker you'll be ignored.

I know what you're thinking—"Four sentences?! No way that can work!" Actually, we've sent thousands of emails like this, and we've seen it work over and over and over again. Trust me: being short and to the point with your cold outreach is the best possible way to actually get responses from the people you want to reach.

2. MAKE IT EASY

OK, this may sound weird, but here it goes: your initial goal is *not* to get your recipient to commit to collaborating with you. That's where many people get it wrong. Instead, your goal is much simpler: get them to respond.

Keep the message short and to the point, and make your call to action outlandishly easy for them to respond to. For example:

> Hi Kim, we're working on an industry blog series and would love to feature you in it. Up for it?
>
> Thanks,
> James Carbary

This type of message will inevitably pique your recipient's curiosity. You're offering something valuable to them (making them look like an industry expert), but you haven't shared any of the details. Instead, you've simply asked if they're interested.

It's easy for someone to respond to this email. Because the email is so short, there's no confusion as to what you're asking them. Since you've made it so easy for them to respond, they likely will.

3. PERSONALIZE YOUR MESSAGES

The more personalized your message is, the more likely someone is to engage with you. The reason is simple: as humans, we like personal contact, whether it comes from a handshake, being called by our name, or a mention of something we're interested in.

Personalization works wonders during outreach—and there are plenty of ways to do it right. For instance, if you're reaching out to someone who spoke at a conference, try this:

Hey Angela,

I saw that you spoke at the Great Big Marketing Conference earlier this year, and I'd love to have you share that content with our podcast listeners. Interested?

Alternatively, you can weave in a specific mention of a recent accomplishment. For instance:

Hey Ethan,

I saw that *Inc.* listed BombBomb as one of the best places to work in the US. We'd love to feature you in our video series to talk about your company culture. Any interest?

Maybe they didn't speak at a conference or get featured in *Inc.*, but they *did* write a LinkedIn article three months ago:

Hey Bill,

I thought your LinkedIn article about productivity hacks was really insightful. I think some of the things you shared there would be really helpful for our blog readers. Any interest in an interview to elaborate on some of the ideas from your article?

Mentioning that you saw someone speak at a conference or read their article brings validity to their work, and it's an ego-stroke for them. Plus, showing that you took the time to learn about them shows you're serious about your content collaboration.

4. WRITE LIKE YOU TALK

Another critical element with outreach emails is to write like you talk. Far too often we try to sound overly professional in our writing. But here's the thing: you're not drafting the Declaration of Independence. You're a human being living in the twenty-first century. Forget the flowery language and get right to the point—and again, always err on the side of brevity.

I like to use the "buddy across the table" test. This helps ensure I'm actually remembering to *write like I talk.* I read through my email and ask if that's how I'd talk to my friend sitting across the table from me at lunch. Try it. With that simple filter, you'll be surprised at what you edit out. For instance, you might start with something like this:

Dear Jim,

I host a well-known, celebrated, and award-winning podcast that gets 160,000 downloads a month, which we're very proud of. We've even had the privilege and honor of interviewing Gary Vaynerchuk and Simon Sinek. I thought this may pique your interest in the show, since you're a subject-matter expert in your field. Would you be interested in joining me?

After you run that through the "buddy across the table"

test, you'll quickly see that this is not only too long-winded and way too "professional and academic" sounding, but it's also all about you. Would your buddy really want to hear you go on and on about yourself? Try something like this instead:

Hey Jim,

I saw the article you wrote on LinkedIn about additive manufacturing a few weeks ago. Would love to have you share some insights from that article on our podcast. Up for it?

Now we're talking.

5. PROVE YOU'RE NOT A SCAM

This one is really important. (But you don't want to overdo it.)

I've seen too many examples of cold outreach that tries to overcompensate for the host's credibility. It can end up backfiring. To prove you're not a scam, you can simply place links to your social profiles in your email signature. That way, the person receiving your email can quickly see that there's a real human on the other side of the screen.

Just make sure you don't link to anything where you go off

the deep end on social media. If people see you ranting about your political agenda on Twitter, they might not want anything to do with you.

6. TAKE A MULTICHANNEL APPROACH

While I've focused the discussion in this chapter on email, you have plenty of other avenues for outreach—like the phone or social media. Different people respond to different types of outreach. Test which ones work for the people you're trying to reach.

Our company is effective at connecting via email, because the people *we're* trying to reach check their email every day. But for you, a better approach might be the phone, LinkedIn, or Twitter, depending on your *goals* and your *people*. Test different channels and track your success. If one isn't working, try another until you figure out what gets you the best results. Most likely, you'll end up with more than one channel that works.

7. FOLLOW-UP

Respectful persistence is a critical ingredient to successful outreach. If I don't get a response to my first email, I send a follow-up two or three days later. If I still don't hear back, I'll send a third and final email three or four days later. Technology is your friend here. If you Google "automated email follow-ups," you'll see a ton of tools that can help automate this process for you.

Keep your follow-ups simple. If your initial outreach was four sentences, your next message should be two. For bonus points, thread your email conversations together so Bill knows what you've said in past messages. There's just no need to go over everything again:

> Hey Bill,
>
> I wanted to circle back on this. Any interest in being featured on the show?

If you still haven't heard back after three or four days, ask one more time:

> Hey Bill,
>
> I haven't heard back from you, but I wanted to follow up one last time. We'd love to feature you on the show. Interested?

When I talk to people about follow-up, the most common response is that they don't want to be annoying. The reality is that you're not being annoying—you're actually being helpful. When I first started following up, I was shocked at how many people thanked me for it. Think about it; you're not trying to hard sell aluminum siding.

You're offering to feature them in content that will make them look like an expert. Who doesn't want that?

With that said, if at any point someone says they're not interested or otherwise asks to be left alone, be like Elsa and let it go. This seems like common sense, but some people just keep at it, and that's when you go from being helpful to being annoying.

DON'T WING IT

The number one goal of Content-Based Networking is to create meaningful relationships with the people who can help you move the needle on your dreams. If you botch the initial outreach, it's over before you even reach the starting line.

> It's not about what they can do for you. It's about what *you* can do for *them*.

Luckily, you'll know pretty quickly if your outreach is working: people respond to you. If they don't, you need to go back to the drawing board—which means heading back to chapter 4 and reconsidering your ideal guest. From there, reevaluate your method of outreach, and most importantly, your message.

Finally, make sure that you're clearly communicating

value to the other person (be like Oprah). While Content-Based Networking is inherently valuable, it's up to *you* to make that value explicit. Remember, it's not about what they can do for you. It's about what you can do for *them*. If you toss in a little Oprah, and check all seven boxes that I just mentioned, the chances are good that you'll see a 30% to 50% reply rate and be well on your way to building relationships with the exact people you want to know.

CHAPTER 8

ALL THE OTHER STUFF OPRAH DID REALLY WELL

I know we've talked a lot about Oprah already. But I hope you're as happy as I am that we aren't done yet. Oprah did a tremendous amount right with her spotlight, so I love to use her as an example.

The benefits of her approach are almost endless, but I've managed to boil them down to a list that explains why that approach is so valuable. Plus, when you can see her process broken down, you may start to get an even better sense of why Content-Based Networking is so valuable.

INDUSTRY EXPERTS KNOW OTHER EXPERTS

We were hinting at this earlier, but now it's time to just go out and say it: A huge benefit of connecting with industry experts, whether or not they give you a job, invest in your company, or help you reach your dreams, is this: People you really want to connect with always have a network of other people...that you also really want to connect with.

The hiring manager you ask to be on your video series likely knows lots of other hiring managers. When you write a blog and feature a music producer, you have to remember—their network is full of *other* music producers. And another benefit is, when you shine the spotlight on someone, they're going to amplify that spotlight by sharing it with as many other people as possible so they can say, "Hey, check out this cool vlog I was featured in."

WHEN YOU STAND WITH EXPERTS, YOU'RE AN EXPERT

Here's a crazy outcome of inserting yourself into a circle of experts—all of a sudden, you're an expert too. For some reason, when people see you with pros, they assume you're one too. (Especially if you're the one with the spotlight.) It's one of the many reasons we know Oprah has so much good advice for life.

> When people see you hanging around the pros, they assume you're one too.

She has a fascinating backstory, one filled with adversity and triumph. While these experiences played a huge part in shaping and honing her charisma, personality, and empathy, they're not the only elements that made her a cultural icon. She created content with various experts, and so when we think of Oprah on just about *any* topic, we think of her as an expert. And frankly, she *is* an expert—not only because of her personal victories, but because of who she's been around her entire career. She's learned firsthand, from some of the most thoughtful, intelligent, and inspiring people alive. She's had rare opportunities to meet some of the most sought-after people on the planet, and by virtue of that, she's gleaned even more.

WHEN YOU INTERVIEW EXPERTS, YOU CAN ASK ANYTHING YOU WANT

I want to be careful here, because you still have to maintain the spotlight effect. The point isn't to highlight you, it's to highlight the person you're collaborating with. But, in all honesty, if you start collaborating on content with some of the greatest minds in your industry, of course you get an opportunity to ask them questions no one else can. And the most amazing part is, when you ask questions in this context, it doesn't sound out of place.

Take my real-life buddy Brandon, for instance.

Brandon is an aspiring real estate investor. He has a clear picture of the types of investments he's looking for—specifically, deals that don't require tons of up-front investment—but he's found these are tricky deals to source.

Hoping to open the door to more opportunities, Brandon started a podcast called *Real Estate for the Rest of Us.* His guests are local real estate investors who've been successful in the market. His goal isn't to sell anything to these investors. Brandon just wants to plug into the local community. Through the network he's building, his hope is that someone will point him to a deal that matches what he's looking for.

I know, I know—I talk a lot about podcasting, but that's not really the point. Because Brandon has a spotlight (media exposure in the form of his podcast), he gets to interview investors and real estate professionals, asking them questions others are scouring the internet for, or even paying for. Brandon doesn't have to do that. If he wants to know a professional's opinion on the real estate market in a specific city, he can do that, and it is a completely normal question in this context.

PRO TIP

This approach is especially helpful if you're looking for your dream job. If you're developing content with hiring managers, you now get to ask them any question you want. Many people would kill to have five minutes with the person responsible for hiring for their dream job. You can't buy that kind of time—you can only gain it by having a spotlight and shining it.

EXPERTS WILL TEACH YOU EVERYTHING ABOUT THE INDUSTRY

Content-Based Networking provides you with a *tremendous* learning opportunity. In the first year of our podcast, we interviewed over 300 guests—providing us with an *invaluable crash course* on B2B marketing from leaders who had been in the trenches for years. Real industry knowledge (the kind you probably won't find inside a university) is only found by spending years on the job or hanging out with other people who've spent years on the job.

If you interview dozens of experts about a subject, you will learn way more than you could have from a book, college course, or a Google search. Trust us.

By applying Oprah's framework of connecting with the experts, we've seen incredible success for our own show, *B2B Growth*. In just 10 months after launching our show, the signs of success were everywhere:

- *B2B Growth* was being downloaded over 30,000 times a month.
- Other high-profile podcasts invited us on as guests.
- *B2B Growth* was mentioned in *Inc.* and *Forbes*.
- PR agencies started introducing us to their clients.

And here's the kicker: This kind of success isn't unique to us—many of our customers have seen similar wins by following a Content-Based Networking approach. By offering your guests a platform to share their expertise, you not only create better content, but you also build trust and attention with your audience. Plus, you get to be like Oprah. And everyone wants to be like Oprah.

FACT: YOU ARE A JOURNALIST

To get the most from Content-Based Networking, you need to see yourself as a journalist. Don't freak out when I say that. I'm not suggesting you need to be the next Oprah. I'm saying we can all learn a lot from her. Oprah embodies the characteristics of a great journalist. She's curious. She's passionate. She's relentlessly focused on sharing incredible content. She connects with people on a human level and draws out their expertise. The good news is, these are actually the qualities of a good journalist. Curiosity, passion, and a focus on great content are what make a journalist a journalist—not fancy equipment.

My friend Lucas does this so well. Lucas owns a construction company that specializes in senior living communities. Instead of taking a traditional business development approach, he has gone all-in on Content-Based Networking. Every year, Lucas and his team attend at least a dozen industry-related conferences, where they set up shop as a senior living podcast called *Bridge the Gap*. Their table is big and eye-catching, and through the attention it creates, they're able to interview the many decision-makers (important people) and thought leaders (other important people) who are attending the conference.

Since Lucas first started taking this approach, I've never heard him say anything about converting his podcast guests into clients. Instead, he takes his role as an industry journalist seriously—and as such, he is relentlessly focused on producing valuable *content*. That dedication has paid off. In less than a year of taking this approach, he and his team have gone from conference curiosities to a can't-miss conference experience. Everybody wants to be a guest on *Bridge the Gap*. People have even stopped Lucas in the halls and asked if they can take selfies with him. Basically, he's the LeBron James of senior living.

Together, Lucas and his podcast guests work together to celebrate the industry and shine a light on the important issues facing it.

Lucas is far from a household name like Oprah. Until you started reading this section, you probably didn't know anything about him. However, within his industry, he's a respected leader who has the ear of decision-makers. And, his show is now sponsored by some of the biggest brands in senior living.

Industry expertise doesn't need to mean worldwide fame. In fact, it rarely does. All you need to do is find a way to collaborate with the specific group of people you want to reach. These people could be senior living operators, plumbing equipment manufacturers, or casting directors. Whoever they are, if you're able to connect with them and produce some truly compelling *content*, then it's a win for everybody.

CHAPTER 9

HOW TO MAKE SURE YOU'RE FINDING THE RIGHT PEOPLE

Sometimes, it takes a try or two to determine who the right people are that can make decisions and help you reach your goals. I know this from experience. We found this out at my company, Sweet Fish, when we initially went after the wrong guests for one of our first podcasts (*B2B Growth*).

Here's how it went down.

Our dream at Sweet Fish is to educate 1 million leaders every single day. Because when leaders learn, the world gets better. To accomplish this dream, we help other companies effectively leverage Content-Based Networking through shows that we own and the shows we produce for our customers. In the early days, we thought the best way to do that was by targeting those companies' chief marketing officers (CMOs) and building relationships with those CMOs. So I decided it would be a good idea to interview a bunch of CMOs, then do a series of articles about them in my *Huffington Post* column.

It sounded like a good idea. But it wasn't.

Spoiler: I was sort of new at this whole Content-Based Networking thing.

On the production side, things went great. Pretty much every CMO I reached out to was on board. I mean, who wouldn't want to share their expertise in *Huffington Post*? Once I'd assembled my group, I asked each CMO a series of 10 to 15 questions and bundled their responses into different articles. The content turned out great, and I had built relationships with each of the CMOs. It seemed like everything was perfect. I had a *goal,* I had managed to connect with those *people,* and we effectively created plenty of *content.* And, this Content-Based Networking thing was working, because I had developed genuine relationships with all these CMOs along the way.

But there was just one problem: *the CMOs weren't the right people.*

It turned out that CMOs weren't the ones who would make buying decisions for what we sell. We should have made our *goal* to connect with VPs of Marketing, not CMOs. The difference may not sound like much, but in this industry, that subtle change made a huge difference.

So, since I was going after the wrong people with the wrong title (CMOs), it wouldn't have mattered what content I produced with them. I could have done articles, podcasts, or a series of interpretive marketing dances. The *content* still wouldn't have mapped to our *goals* because we weren't talking to the right people.

Now, on the one hand, Content-Based Networking honestly still worked. By developing relationships with the CMOs, even though they weren't actually my ideal people, I was able to learn really quickly who the people were that I *did* need to develop relationships with. So, honestly, I still counted it as a win, but I did have to make some adjustments to find the right people.

While you may not be trying to sell your marketing service to tech companies, you still want to get as close to the right people as possible when you start with Content-Based Networking. Having helped lots of other companies implement Content-Based Networking, I have a few ideas on how to get you to the right people and eliminate some of the trial and error.

TARGET EXPERTS, NOT CELEBRITIES

B2B Growth has produced over 1,000 episodes, featuring interviews with a variety of marketing leaders. Yes, we've had big names like Gary Vaynerchuk and Simon Sinek on our show, and yes, we use those names as credibility indicators to help attract other guests to our show. But ultimately, those big-name interviews aren't what the podcast is all about. In fact, they're not even our most listened-to episodes.

> Influencers will only get you so far.

The truth is, our listeners will only gain so much from the big-picture thought leadership that people like GaryVee and Simon Sinek provide. We've cultivated an audience of professionals who are in the trenches. They need practical, actionable advice—and the best place to get that advice is from practitioners who are in the trenches with them, not from big names who have tons of Instagram followers.

Influencers will only get you so far. Plus, here's the other thing to consider: The GaryVee of your world has very little reason to be excited about coming on your show, and probably even less reason to share it. However, when you invite an expert who's passionate about a topic but rarely receives the limelight, they'll share their episode with everyone they can.

DON'T MAKE IT ABOUT YOU

Another mistake people make is branding the show around them or their company instead of their guests. For instance, if our show was called *The Sweet Fish Media Podcast* instead of *B2B Growth*, nobody would listen to it. People don't care about our company. But, people *do* care about growing their business, so we branded our show around our *people,* and called it *B2B Growth*.

Another great example is my friend Sharon Toerek, who's an attorney.

Sharon has built her entire legal practice around working with marketing agency owners. So, she has made it a *goal* to connect with agency owners, because they will ultimately be the ones buying Sharon's legal services.

So, to connect with those agency owners, Sharon started a podcast called *The Innovative Agency*. Notice the title doesn't say *anything* about law. You know why? Because law is what Sharon does, but it's not what her clients do. They honestly aren't very interested in law (which is exactly why they need someone like Sharon). But, agency owners—the people Sharon wants to connect with—*are* interested in having a better *marketing agency*.

Sharon created a show centered on that idea—helping agency owners build an innovative marketing agency.

On every episode, Sharon invites agency owners to share innovative ideas, their struggles, and what they've learned that can help other agency owners. She doesn't drill them with questions about legal issues.

Sharon's approach is an extremely effective way to provide value to both your guests and to your audience, but, there's another benefit to you as well. When you make your *content* about your guests rather than about you, you gain invaluable insights.

Like we said earlier, when you have someone on your show, you can ask them anything. Sharon doesn't need to guess what legal issues agency owners are having. She can just ask them! Even if none of the guests decide to immediately work with Sharon, she still benefits by learning more about the community she serves.

THAT ABOUT DOES IT FOR STEP 2: *PEOPLE*.

Just to sum it up, you want to be a spotlight. Please don't make that harder than it really is. To be a spotlight, you just pick one up, and then shine it on your industry and specifically on the people you are trying to connect with. If it takes you a couple tries to figure out the right people, no sweat. Just keep at it.

Oh yeah, and, as always, be like Oprah.

CONTENT

CHAPTER 10

HERE'S WHAT YOU TALK ABOUT

Reader: James, I'm sold on this idea of Content-Based Networking, so I'm starting a content series featuring the people I need to connect with. But, how the heck do I know what to talk about?!

Me: I have no idea what to talk about in your content. (But your guests do.)

We've talked a lot about Oprah. But I also hope you've been able to understand your *goals*—the connections you are trying to make. And I hope you've learned some valuable information about *people*—and how to get them to engage with you.

Now, we're at the final step of Content-Based Networking: *content*.

Earlier, we said to just get started. Maybe a few of you immediately started a blog, a podcast, or vlog, but my guess is, most of you want to finish this book before diving in headfirst.

I totally understand that.

This section of the book will help you determine more of the nitty-gritty of content collaboration. And, the very first place you want to start is with the individuals you're trying to connect with.

Do you remember the earlier story about Patrick? If you don't, here's the scoop: Patrick started a podcast about CLOs (Chief Learning Officers) called *The CLO Show.*

Now, let me tell you a secret about Patrick's show. Patrick really didn't have any idea what CLOs talk about.

Patrick was in the same place a lot of you reading this may find yourselves—once you've determined your hyperfocused *goal,* which revolves around *people,* then you know it's time to start developing *content.*

But there's just one issue: you aren't quite sure what to make your *content* about.

Well, that's where Patrick found himself. He started a show *about* CLOs, but he wasn't sure what to talk about.

But you know who does know what CLOs like to talk about, what they do on a day-to-day basis, and what their career journeys look like?

CLOs.

Instead of trying to come up with subject matter, Patrick just went straight to where CLOs hang out (which is apparently at CLO conferences). He shook hands, smiled big, talked to people, and asked multiple people at these events if they'd like to be featured on his podcast, *The CLO Show*. Patrick didn't have a list of in-depth questions to ask them, and he didn't have a huge audience yet. But that didn't stop him. Guess what? Patrick didn't hear, "How many people download your show?" "How much of an expert are you?" or "Are you even a CLO?" Mostly, people just said, "Sure, I'd love to be on your show!"

Along the way, Patrick discovered everything he needed to know about CLOs, and then he parlayed that information into his next interview. Since he wasn't the expert about CLO life, he just talked to CLOs about what they did and their background (at first). And he learned along the way about the challenges and opportunities that CLOs think about every day. Every time he spoke with one CLO, he had a clearer picture of their world, the things CLOs struggle with, what they care about, what information is helpful to them, things they don't care about, etc. He then started to leverage all that new knowledge with the next interview guest (another CLO), and asked better, more specific questions as he continued to understand more and more about the life of a CLO.

> Instead of trying to come up with subject matter, let your guests take the lead.

In a relatively short amount of time, Patrick *became* an expert. And it didn't take a master's degree from a fancy school. He got a master class on corporate learning and development from the best possible source: Chief Learning Officers.

Now, Patrick knows a thing or two about this industry. He can ask increasingly thoughtful, detailed, and specific questions to each interviewee. And this expertise keeps deepening as Patrick does more and more interviews.

The same thing will happen to you as you do your interviews. You'll learn so much about the industry because you are doing the journalistic work that nobody else is doing. Soon, you'll be the person curating data and sharing interesting insights. It's pretty fun to see how this turns around *very* quickly. After diving deep into an industry with your interviews, your guests will start asking *you* questions about problems they're having. And why not? Who would know better about this topic than the person who's been interviewing all the experts about it?

PRO TIP

One time in the early days of *B2B Growth*, I had a guest who spent a good chunk of our interview talking about category creation. I had no idea what he was talking about. (If I'm being honest, it was probably another year *after* that conversation until I finally did.) But it didn't matter because *he* did.

I know it can feel a little nerve-wracking to be in a situation like this, where you feel like you're just playing along even though you have no idea what your guest is talking about. If you find yourself in a situation like this, here's a tip: the verbiage you use to ask questions matters.

If you don't know what your guest is talking about, your audience might not either. So, if there's a particular point that's going over your head or there's something you're just not understanding, advocate for your audience. Say something like, "For our listeners who aren't as familiar with this concept, could you walk us through exactly what category creation means?"

Pay attention to enough interviews, and you'll see hosts do this all the time. It's a great pivot and a useful strategy. Not only do you get a chance to learn (without giving away that you don't know what your guest is talking about), but you're also advocating for your audience, which gives you more authority as an interviewer.

CHAPTER 11

THE THREE PHASES OF COLLABORATION

Hopefully that last chapter helped you understand that you don't have to be an expert to start.

You just have to interview the experts (and start!).

Now I want to go a little deeper and give you some practical tips on how to create great *content*.

What makes content collaboration so powerful is that it's *action-oriented*. And that's exactly how this chapter is going to be, so buckle up.

This isn't an exceptionally long chapter, and the advice in here isn't especially complicated. But it's crucial that you get collaboration right. Without it, Content-Based Networking probably won't work for you.

THE 3 PHASES OF BUILDING RELATIONSHIPS

This is barely newsworthy, but here it goes: Building any meaningful relationship requires time and multiple interactions. This is true in business, in friendship, and even in love. For instance, even though I was convinced that I'd met my future wife the night I met Lisa, we didn't get married right there on the spot. I assume that's because we weren't on a reality TV show. We also didn't get married after our first date—or for many dates after. Believe it or not, I am a *little* smoother than that. I knew Lisa and I needed to build a strong relationship based on multiple interactions in order to work up to that kind of commitment.

When you do Content-Based Networking right, the *content* paves the way for multiple interactions. These multiple interactions build the relationship, making it stronger and stronger as you go. There will be many touchpoints along the way when you do Content-Based Networking the right way, but, generally, everything falls into three phases:

1. Plan
2. Create
3. Share

Throughout these three phases, you'll form a genuine relationship with your guests. This three-part framework often leaves the door open for more collaborations in the future as well.

> Building any meaningful relationship requires time and multiple interactions. This is true in business, in friendship, and even in love.

Oh, one quick thing to point out as we move through these phases. I want you to notice that I never said, "Here's how to sell," or "Use this to ask for favors." Relationships aren't built that way. Building relationships is genuine, fun, interesting, and totally normal.

1. PLAN

Content-Based Networking begins as soon as a guest agrees to creating *content* with you.

There are actually quite a few small pieces you'll need to get in order, like scheduling and logistics. So, make it easy for your guest, and handle all the small stuff for them. I made a quick guide to help with this:

DON'T ASK FOR TOO MUCH

I see a lot of people mess up the initial communication by

asking for *way* too much, *way* too early. Often, as soon as someone says yes to collaborating, people get so excited about the content, they send over a giant questionnaire, they ask for headshots, send an email requesting a bio, etc. Whoa. That's a lot.

Once you've asked your guest for something simple (i.e., "Hey, wondering if you're interested in being on our podcast?"), don't follow it up by asking for their social security number. It's too much, too soon. Instead, focus on what you can do to make the experience as easy as possible for them, and keep the requests for information to a minimum. Just be excited they said yes. (There'll be plenty of time for more questions later.)

MAKE SCHEDULING A BREEZE

Make it as easy as possible for your guest. You may be meeting in-person, over the phone, or via video.

Regardless of how you're connecting to create the *content*, there are lots of tools you can use to make the scheduling as seamless as possible (I really like Calendly).

PRO TIP

Make sure you have all the tools you'll need to record your interviews (video, mic, etc.), but don't overthink the equipment—we find a lot of people spend way too much time, money, and effort on gear. That's not what we're advocating for. We're just saying that if you're going to need a mic, get a mic. If you need recording software, make sure you have it.

DETERMINE AHEAD OF TIME WHAT TOPICS YOU'LL BE COVERING

Once you have scheduling worked out, set some objectives. Remember, approach your *content* like a journalist and ask these questions as you consider what you and your guest will be discussing:

- What's the overall theme of the *content* you'll be creating?
- What tangible takeaways will your audience walk away with after consuming this *content*?

In my experience, people often struggle with that last point—tangible takeaways. While the overall goal of Content-Based Networking is to develop relationships with the guests, why leave your audience out of the picture? And, just so we're clear about what your audience wants, trust me, 9 times out of 10, they want actionable takeaways they can immediately implement.

Your audience wants to walk away and be able to do something. So keep your *content* focused on what your audience can do after they are finished consuming your *content*. Ask yourself: "At the end of this discussion, what could a reader/listener/viewer immediately do with this information?"

BE SPECIFIC (AND USE AN OUTLINE)

This is similar to the earlier point about having tangible takeaways. As a rule, specificity works really well. It helps everyone follow the *content*, it saves time, and it allows your guests to focus on their area of expertise and what they are trying to communicate.

Let's say you are going to do a video series about architecture, and you and your guest are going to talk about how architects can be more productive. Perfect. Use that. But you can also draw the lines a little narrower to help your guest out, especially if they're a little nervous about the interview. Just say something like this: "Do you have three things that help you stay productive?" By narrowing down the topic to three major productivity tips, you've made it easier for your guest to focus on the *content* (not the camera), and now, it will be easier for you to lead the interview, since you both have a compass to guide the conversation.

One of the best ways to keep the conversation specific (and on-topic, so no one goes off on tangents), is to use an outline. This is especially important if you're doing an interview. Beforehand, jot down a few questions you'll be asking your guest and the three to five takeaways you want the audience to have by the end. Then go over your outline with the guest right before the interview, ask for their input, and adjust accordingly.

PRO TIP

Here's a great way to determine the specifics of your *content*: use any material your guest has already produced. By doing your homework, you can find out about a conference they spoke at, an article they wrote, or even something they posted on social media. These all act as starting points. That way, all you have to do is say, "Hey, I saw that you shared something about how to find better talent in your industry. Care to elaborate on that?"

BE FLEXIBLE

Always allow for flexibility within the interview—the specificity is there to help drive the conversation, tease the interests of your audience, and help your guest deliver without nervousness. But if the conversation develops into something else interesting (which it *often* does), let the conversation wander. It's OK. Again, remember, your primary goal is to build a relationship; the specificity just helps get the ball rolling.

Picture the topics as ice breakers with your guest, with the objective of creating fun, organic conversations. If the conversation goes *way* off track, you can always bring it back, or just edit your *content.*

BE MINDFUL OF EVERYONE'S TIME

Most content collaboration doesn't need to take up too much time. We find that 20 to 30 minutes is usually enough. It's rare for anyone to watch or listen to a one-hour piece of educational content on just about anything. So try to keep the content inside of 30 minutes. Just do a few minutes of homework before your meetup with the other person, and you should be able to hone the topics enough to get good content in a few minutes.

Of course, sometimes, your guest will be having so much fun, *they* want to keep the conversation going—that's great. Go for it. But don't expect that.

PRO TIP

Record everything. Trust us on this one. This is a huge timesaver. Even if you're hopping on a phone call just to ask a few questions for a blog or e-book, go ahead and record the call. This helps avoid embarrassing follow-up questions that have already been answered, plus, often, you'll discover things you didn't catch the first time around.

2. CREATE

Since you're the one with the spotlight, your guest is going to be leaning on you for guidance. (It's actually pretty interesting how much credibility people immediately give you when you simply say, "I host a podcast about XYZ.") A lot of your guests may feel a little nervous when a mic is in front of them or when they know their words will end up online somewhere. So, to produce effective, compelling content, you need to be in the driver's seat.

Without a little guidance, many guests will default to talking about their personal career, or all the amazing things their company has done—neither of which is likely to be of much interest to your audience. Others simply won't know what to say. So you get to help them find the interesting story to tell. And everyone has a compelling story. They just need help finding it sometimes. Finding that story becomes easier with every interview, but if the interviewing process is new for you, I have four pieces of advice.

LEARN FROM OTHERS

Whatever type of content you're planning to produce, someone else has likely already talked about it. Don't steal, but commandeer their ideas, as Captain Jack would say.

BE CURIOUS

Ask lots of questions. The tendency is to think that your guests will get annoyed when you say, "Can you break that down a little more?" The opposite is true. Your guest, who's an expert, has dedicated a lot of their lives to this subject, and they're excited to be talking about it.

HAVE FUN

Seriously, if all else fails, make this fun. It's OK to ask about their favorite music, their family, or for any of their hidden talents—here's the deal, everyone likes talking about themselves. So give them that opportunity.

DON'T LOSE SIGHT OF YOUR GOAL

The whole purpose of Content-Based Networking is to build genuine relationships with your guests. Be smart with your questions and the way you engage. This is more about serving and highlighting your guest than it is about you.

PRO TIP

Don't try to sell anything or promote yourself when you're creating content with your guests. But hey, there's nothing wrong with laying down some groundwork while you're talking to them. If you can do so organically and in a way that's relevant to the conversation, feel free to ask questions that may be helpful for you down the road.

For example, if you're an actor, you could phrase one of your questions like this: "Well, Frank, I'm an actor, and I've interviewed a lot of casting directors, and one of the things they tell me is that it's hard to find people who will simply take directions. Do you have that same struggle, and how have you dealt with it?" Questions like this are valuable to your audience and interesting to your guests (who also now knows that you're an actor).

The big idea here is authenticity. It's OK to be up-front about what you do as long as you put it in the context of your conversation. If you turn your interview into a sales call or self-promotion in disguise, your guests will see straight through that.

3. SHARE

In the eyes of your guests, you're a content creator, a journalist, and an influencer—a committed professional working to add value to the community. This is good news for you, because while no one wants to hear a sales pitch, they *do* want their expertise featured in the media and shared with the world. The reality of Content-Based Networking is that once you start down this path, you're no longer just a jobseeker, an entrepreneur, or an aspiring actor. You're a media entity.

So live up to that title. See your collaborations through. Use them to create compelling content, and then share that content with the world.

Here are a few tips on sharing content.

JUST FINISH IT

If you only get one thing right, get this right: Publish. Finish. Hit "upload." Post on social media. We would borrow three little words from our friends at Nike, but apparently they're trademarked. So just finish it. The final product doesn't have to win an Oscar or a National Book Award, but it *does* need to be available for the world to see. Way too many people never upload their content because they get wrapped up in having a perfectly edited final product. That's not the point. But sharing the content *is* the point. It's far more important to have content than to have perfect content.

MAKE YOUR CONTENT EASY TO CONSUME

The average person will give you *seconds* of their attention before they're on to the next piece of content. If they have to jump through hoops, download a special media player, or view it on their computer rather than their mobile device, forget it. They've moved on. Make your content as simple as possible to consume. Then go back over it, and make sure it's easier. If it takes *any* real work to read, watch, or listen to your content, you are definitely losing people.

BE EXCITED

Tell your guest how awesome it was to work with them and how stoked you are that the content is now up for the world to see. Whether you're excited or disappointed with the outcome, your response acts like a self-fulfilling prophecy: people who are excited about content usually inspire others to check it out, who are then going into it *looking* for something valuable they can take away—and then, hopefully, share it with someone else.

* * *

I hope two things really stood out for you in this chapter:

1. Just finish.
2. Make it fun.

If only two things happen, let it be those two. Posting your content and having a laugh along the way—if those are the only takeaways you and your guest have, it's a huge win.

Everything else is icing on the cake.

CHAPTER 12

PRODUCE, REUSE, RECYCLE (HOW 1 = 3)

Another short chapter alert. This chapter isn't long, and it doesn't need to be. The point I'm going to make is pretty clear:

One collaboration is never just one piece of content.

This is a pretty easy concept.

But a lot of things in life are simple, and that doesn't make them any less crucial. Wearing deodorant is *also* a simple concept, and would likely also be a short chapter in the *How to Get a Second Date* book, but it's still important.

So let's get to it.

1 = 3

Every time you do an interview or collaborate with some-one on *anything,* that collaboration should become *at least* three pieces of content.

Sorry, but I've got to talk about GaryVee again (he's the entrepreneur I mentioned earlier). No one pro-duces, reuses, and recycles content better than Gary. In the world of entrepreneurship and marketing, he's an extremely sought-after speaker. He travels all around the globe—Dubai, Los Angeles, Sydney, Sao Paulo—to share his thoughts. When he delivers his keynote speeches, he records them. Then, he turns that one-hour speech into dozens of shorter two-minute video clips, some ten-minute video clips, Instagram posts, LinkedIn videos, etc. From one piece of content (a speech), he can create over *thirty pieces of content.* You may be thinking: "But I don't give keynote speeches." Well, first of all, you may not give keynote speeches *yet.* But you may soon. I'd never given a speech either until I started interviewing experts... and then *bam:* I started being seen as an expert as well. When people see you as an expert, offers to speak start rolling in.

But even if you're not giving keynote speeches yet, here's the deal: if you are interviewing *another* expert, that's a fantastic opportunity to create different types of content, like videos, quotes, or articles. It's pretty simple to do (we literally do it *every day* at Sweet Fish). We take the podcast interview and we find a few great quotes and sound bites. The sound bites become teasers for the podcast. We turn the quotes into graphics (which makes them easier to put on certain social media platforms). Then, we create a social media post from one or two of the main ideas our guest brought up. Then we write a blog article. Then, we create a short summary of the interview, which can be turned into a description for podcast channels like Apple Podcasts and Spotify. It's *work*, but it's not rocket science. Anyone who interviews guests has lots of content.

You'll probably figure out endless ways to repurpose content from your collaborations, but here are a few ideas to get the ball rolling.

1. DON'T WAIT FOR THE MONA LISA

I know we said this earlier—but just get your content out there. You don't have to polish everything until it's perfect. It's more important to get a quote, a LinkedIn status update, or a blog post published then it is to make sure you have all the commas in the right place.

2. NO LIGHTS. NO CAMERA. JUST ACTION

You already have the spotlight. It's time to skip the fluff and make your content actionable. Set your guest up to share something that your audience can take immediate action on.

3. BE ALEXANDER HAMILTON (AND DON'T BE AARON BURR)

Have you seen the Broadway hit *Hamilton*? If not, no worries. I'll catch you up on what you need to know for this conversation.

Hamilton stood up for what he believed, regardless of which way the popular tide flowed. Burr waited to see where the river would run, and once he was sure, he just let the current take him with it.

Spoiler: The musical is about Alexander Hamilton. Not Aaron Burr.

Here's the deal: Many people will tell you not to say anything controversial, to make no one upset, to cause no ripples and no waves. I don't believe in seeking out controversy or trying to rock the boat simply for rocking the boat's sake. But, if you take what you originally wanted to say, and then strip it of anything that may possibly offend one person somewhere in the world, you are going to end up saying nothing.

So say something.

If you publish content, put a stake in the ground. Make a choice. Is there a disagreement in your industry? It's OK to offer a fresh perspective or say why you believe what you believe. You can always change your mind later.

In the moment, it always sounds best to just go with the flow. Fast-forward to the end of your life, and you'll have moved no one, changed nothing, and been completely forgettable. The truth is, you have something to offer. So offer it.

4. BEYONCÉ IS YOUR FRIEND

People either love Beyoncé or hate her. But guess what? Everyone's heard of her. We use pop culture references all the time—even in the sometimes-boring world of B2B. It's OK. In fact, people like it.

If you are creating a video series about architecture, use something that recently popped up in the news when you repurpose the content.

Here's how we do this at Sweet Fish: Every week we send out an email called the *B2B Growth Big 3* that highlights our podcast interviews from the week before. (See how we found *another way* to repurpose our content?!) We take three ideas from three episodes and use a pop culture reference to drive that point home.

For example, one week, we designed the entire email around a really popular TV show that had just released a new season (*Stranger Things*). No one on any of our podcasts had mentioned anything about the show. That's OK. We just took their original ideas and made a reference to something about *Stranger Things* that aligned with their topic. Another week, we titled our email "3 Marketing Ideas That Will Never Work in the Gym (But They're Great for B2B)." Why? Health and fitness is *in*. Everyone's already talking about it, so we are too. Even though our audience is made up of B2B marketing professionals, they can resonate with a reference to the gym.

The point is this: When you're repurposing content, use pop culture as your friend to engage your audience and make the content current and relevant. Reference Beyoncé. Talk about the Super Bowl. It's OK if it wasn't in the original piece of content.

5. RE-HIGHLIGHT YOUR NEW FRIEND

When you're repurposing content, use it as an opportunity to shine that spotlight right back onto your new friend. You don't have to be weird about it—sometimes we just post on social media with a simple, "Here's a great thought from our recent interview with Angela!" What we always do, though, is tag them and credit them. One, everyone loves to be praised. Two, often, when you give someone else credit, they're more inclined to share that post. Three, external validation is always better for everyone—when you say, "Here's this person's great idea," you sound much better than if you say, "I'm awesome. Here's what I think."

6. REMEMBER YOUR TARGET AUDIENCE (REVERSE ENGINEER WHAT *THEY* ARE INTERESTED IN)

Remember: content isn't about you. During the interview process, it's mostly about the person you are interviewing. You want to build that relationship. When you're pushing out content, you want to continue to highlight that individual and you also want to drive increased awareness around that primary piece of content you created. So, think about what your audience is interested in, and when you repurpose that primary content in other formats, throw in something that you know will excite and interest *them*.

PRO TIP

Come on, you just got an entire chapter full of six pro tips. Do you really need a seventh?

* * *

All right, now you know how to produce, reuse, and recycle content. But the most important thing isn't *how* you repurpose content. It's that you just make it happen.

Never let one interview become just one piece of content.

CHAPTER 13

THE RELATIONSHIP SNOWBALL

I assume everyone reading this has seen the movie *Field of Dreams*. (And, if you haven't seen *Field of Dreams*, go watch it right now. Your happiness in life will increase by at least 20%. Fact.)

OK, *now* that everyone has seen *Field of Dreams*, here's the comparison to relationships—relationships are like the ballpark in the movie: if you build them, the reward will come. And your collaboration—the interview you did with someone, the blog post you collaborated on, or the podcast you featured someone in—is the start of a great relationship.

But no great relationship starts and ends with one date (even if that date was out of this world). The better that first date, the more you want to invest in each other.

Collaboration is like that first date—it's the magic key that opens a giant padlocked door that everyone is struggling to get past. But after you've unlocked that giant door, you still have to walk through it.

> Relationships are like the ballpark in *Field of Dreams:* if you build them, the reward will come.

If you spend all your time and resources finding the magic key and unlocking the door, you're missing out on a phenomenal new relationship after all the hard work is already finished. After several years of successfully applying Content-Based Networking, here's what I can tell you: if you invest in your new relationships that started with a content collaboration, it's like you're adding rocket fuel to a ship. You already created a huge rocket ship (the relationship) by creating content with that person. Now, add the rocket fuel by continuing to invest in the relationship.

Here's how you add that rocket fuel.

1. GRAB A BITE TO EAT

I love face time—the real kind, not the app. Nothing can take the place of being in the same room with someone to share conversation, hear the inflection in their voice, and share a laugh.

I've found that sharing a meal with someone is great for this. So, what I do is keep a list of everyone I've collaborated with and where they're from. If I'm ever in their area, I take them out to eat.

For example, if I'm headed to a conference in Boston, I'll search through my list of guests who are in the area. Then, I'll schedule either a group dinner or, if I have a little more time, a handful of one-on-one meals. Even if your guest has only interacted with you once or twice in the past, most are very receptive to these kinds of invites. And why not? It brings a rewarding return: you get to eat (which everyone has to do anyway), and it offers a rare chance to connect with someone in person.

There's really nothing that will add more rocket fuel to your relationship than food. I don't quite know what it is about food, but it's magical. So share a meal with your guest and watch the relationship flourish.

2. MAKE IT FACEBOOK OFFICIAL

The more ways you can connect with your guests, the more opportunities you'll have to remain top of mind and deepen your relationship. Luckily, today's plugged-in world makes it easy to reengage friends on social media. Platforms like LinkedIn, Twitter, Facebook, and Instagram are all great ways to stay connected.

Each social media platform is a little different. LinkedIn, for instance, is great for professional conversations, but that doesn't mean a more informal platform like Facebook is off limits. Personally, I enjoy connecting with guests from our podcast on Facebook. It gives me a peek into their world, helps me identify common interests, and lets me understand them in another context of their life. Facebook also notifies me when it's their birthday and helps me see special occasions like the announcement of a new baby or an anniversary. Seeing something personal like that on Facebook or Instagram, then sending them a thoughtful note or gift in the mail, goes a long way to build depth into your relationship with them.

PRO TIP

When connecting through digital channels, don't forget that the point here is to be a real human being. Don't get too caught up thinking about what platform to connect through, what kinds of messages you're going to send, or anything like that. Go with what feels natural to the relationship and take it from there.

3. GIVE A GIFT

Everyone likes gifts—that is, as long as the gift is thoughtful.

We've all received generic birthday cards from our dentists or financial advisors. It's nice to know they're thinking of us—and certainly it took some effort to sign a bunch of cards—but the impact is minimal at best. You can do better than that.

If you're new to gift-giving, check out the book *Giftology* by gift-giving expert (and *B2B Growth* guest!) John Ruhlin. Read that thing cover to cover, and I promise you won't regret it. In the meantime, here are a few basic tips.

First, don't treat gifts as a branding opportunity. We've all received the buckets of swag with the gift-giver's logo stamped on everything. Sometimes those things can be nice, but more often than not, they're off-putting.

This brings us to our second tip. Instead of branding every gift you send out, make the gift about *them*. John (the author) likes to send really nice knife sets with the recipient's name engraved on them. How useful is that? I mean, who doesn't need a good set of knives? Plus, knives are something the recipient will likely see every day, reminding them of you. At Sweet Fish, we've sent out gifts like personalized bobbleheads and even customized letterman jackets, but one of my favorite go-to gifts is a pair of Apple AirPods. They're so practical and useful, and they offer a nice, subtle reminder of our company every time someone uses them.

PRO TIP

Don't be afraid to get creative and fun with your gifts. With new customers, we send personalized paintings. We had an artist create a template with famous talk show hosts Oprah, Jimmy Fallon, and Ellen DeGeneres. Then, using that template, we add our customer's face into the image. A caption at the bottom reads, "The new host with the most." Finally, to cap off the effort, we time our gift to be delivered shortly after their first podcast episode has gone live.

4. DO ANOTHER COLLABORATION

If that first content collaboration went well, you can always do another one. We have found this to be incredibly useful. It builds on the previous connection, reengages the relationship, and often, for whatever reason, the magic happens the second time around.

Sometimes it makes sense to immediately dive into another content idea. Other times, it makes sense to wait a while before asking. For instance, if the collaboration goes well, you may want to invite them to work with you again right away. Just say, "Hey, I think this went really well. I'd love to work with you again. Here's another content project we're working on. Can we set up another time to talk about how you can be a part of it?"

Maybe you want to play the more cautious route and wait until your first collaboration is published. If they enjoyed working with you—and if they see that you produced something valuable—they'll gladly respond to that second request to collaborate.

In my experience, that's the beauty of the snowball effect: the more your new friends work with you, the more comfortable they become, and the more likely they are to say yes to other opportunities. And why wouldn't they? To have someone take an active interest in who we are, what we do, and our expertise, is a rare and intriguing concept.

PRO TIP

Another collaboration is a great way to build a deeper relationship with someone, but make sure the content builds on a new topic. It could be an exploration of something that was quickly mentioned in your last interview, or an entirely new topic, but the main thing is this—don't do the same interview.

HERE'S WHAT HAPPENS WHEN THAT RELATIONSHIP SNOWBALL GAINS STEAM

OK, so let's put it all together.

Let's say you did your first collaboration with Drew, who's in Atlanta, and it was a video collaboration where you interviewed him about his expertise. Of course, you shined your spotlight well and made Drew seem like the genius that he is. All in all, it was a great first interaction, but you're not content to leave it at that.

To deepen that relationship, you decide to organize a dinner in Atlanta, bringing Drew together with a handful of other leaders that you've featured in your YouTube series. Suddenly, you've got a second interaction in the works. Your initial collaboration required a low bar of commitment, just 15 to 20 minutes of time over a video call. This dinner requires a greater commitment of Drew. But since you've invested in the relationship, and because he'll get the chance to connect with other leaders in Atlanta, he wants to go to dinner. Of course, you also connected with Drew on social media, and, through Facebook, you learn that Drew has a daughter, Emily, who's in college. At the dinner, you ask Drew how his daughter Emily is doing with her classes. After dinner, maybe you send Drew a gift, a tee shirt featuring Emily's school.

You and Drew now have a much deeper relationship.

The snowball effect of this approach can't be overstated. I've seen it work too many times to ignore. In fact, some of my best friends have come as a result of this process. They began as someone I wanted to meet, they segued into becoming a regular guest, and eventually they grew into a close friend. I ended up doing business with some of them, and with others I didn't. Either way, I bene-fited tremendously.

B2B SALES

If you aren't in B2B sales, this part of the book may be a little yawn-worthy, so you may want to skip to the next chapter. But, trust me: if you *are* in B2B sales, this section could be exactly what you need. I'm going to use some businessy language here, so here it goes:

So much of the traditional approach to B2B sales just doesn't work anymore. "This is what our product does, and we think you should buy it." To a certain degree, this system works—it's not like decision-makers aren't buying anything from B2B companies. However, this approach does very little for long-term relationships.

Look, I get it: You need to sell stuff to keep the lights on. But you also need relationships to create long-term returns. The traditional hard sell isn't a great way to build long-term relationships. No one wants to be treated like a lead. They want to be treated like a human being. This means that, even after the collaboration, your goal should be to *give*, not to take. If you flip on the sales switch during your interview and start pitching your product, you will create zero opportunities for yourself. You'll end the relationship before it's even had a chance to begin, and you'll have zero fun in the process.

Focusing on relationships makes financial sense too. In B2B sales, the lifetime value of a customer value can end up somewhere between $25,000 and $10,000,000. Decision-makers don't give up that kind of budget easily, and they will only spend it on something they truly need. The more you focus on building friendships rather than driving sales, the more receptive your buyers will be to hearing what you do—which includes referring others who might have a need.

THAT'S THE END OF STEP 3: *CONTENT*

Hopefully, you realized you don't have to be an expert, you can simply shine your spotlight on the expertise of your guests. I hope you also learned that you don't need to be fancy with your content...you just need to get started. Don't forget that every piece of content is really (at least) three pieces of content and lastly... be a snowballer.

Well, that's it. You just finished reading all three steps in Content-Based Networking. But you don't want to miss the next section (I'm a little biased, but there's some pretty good stuff in there).

STEP 4

YOU'RE DONE

CHAPTER 14

SO, AFTER I'VE CREATED ALL THIS CONTENT, DO MY DREAMS JUST MAGICALLY COME TRUE?

You've done everything I've mentioned so far: You established your *goals*, you identified the *people* you need to connect with, and you created *content* with those people. (Hopefully, you also produced, reused, and recycled that content.)

So...now what?

Do all your dreams suddenly become true? Often, yes, actually: they *will* start to come true. By the time you've repurposed some content, created strategic relationships, and learned more about your industry than you could ever imagine, you'll likely be seeing results. Maybe you were offered *more* than one job. Maybe you sold more than you hoped for. Maybe you realized something interesting about your field. Maybe you even developed a new interest or discovered a new ambition. Often, your objectives happen just like that—organically—simply because you put yourself in a position to win. You surrounded yourself with the people you needed to connect with, and *great things* happened.

That's because of a simple truth, which, when expressed, goes something like this: "If you hang around the barbershop long enough, you're going to get a haircut."

Maybe you haven't heard that expression, but you've probably heard, "If you play with fire, you're going to get burned." The idea is the same in both mantras. When you're in and around anything for long enough, it will affect you. So, hang out at the barbershop of casting directors long enough, they're bound to give you a haircut (or, in this case, an acting job). If you hang out at the barbershop of dolphin trainers long enough, you're bound to end up in the water petting a dolphin. It's almost impossible not to.

Content-Based Networking will almost certainly work *eventually*. Just keep at it, keep putting yourself in the barbershop, and you'll get a haircut.

But remember that Content-Based Networking is all about making things happen *on purpose,* which means there are some ways you *can* speed up the process. You may not have to—you may be reaping all the benefits of Content-Based Networking so quickly that you're having a hard time keeping up with all the new opportunities that are showing up in front of you. That happens. But other times, you may want to give it a little push. So, here's another story that may help you out.

THE EARLY DAYS OF *B2B GROWTH*

When I first started our show, *B2B Growth,* I was petrified to ask our guests if they would have any interest in working with us. I cared deeply about the relationships I'd built. I worried that the second I made an offer, my guest would decide the whole thing had been a sham and refuse to speak to me again.

I was way off.

In reality, most people were relieved to hear that Sweet Fish offered a solution to their problem. Most people didn't even know what we did—they saw me only as a journalist, someone with a spotlight. They didn't see me as a businessperson with a service to sell. This was a real eye-opener, and it taught me two big lessons:

1. Make sure your guests know what business you're in (or what your expertise is) as early in the process as possible.
2. When people know, like, and trust you, they're *excited* about the opportunity to work with you.

Essentially, if you've applied the Content-Based Networking framework correctly, all the hard work is already done. You've provided value to the other person first. Likely, (unless this book ends up selling more copies than the Harry Potter books), no one else will have done what you did. Other people with similar *goals* as yours probably took a much different approach. They either took no action at all and simply relied on *hope* for a great opportunity to fall in their lap. Or they reached out to lots of people that could potentially help them, offered no up-front value, and simply asked for what they wanted.

You didn't do that.

By starting with content collaboration, you created value in a way that made your guests excited to engage with you.

Think about it this way: Let's say you're in the *other* person's shoes for a minute. Let's say you're the head football coach at a high school, and you were just asked to come on a podcast to talk about the joys of influencing young men's lives through coaching. The person who interviewed you tells you they're also interested in coaching one day, and if you have any tips for them or know of any open positions where they would be a good fit to let them know. It doesn't feel weird in the least. I know, because I *have been* the other person, and that exact thing happened to me.

(OK, well, it wasn't *exactly* what happened to me. I've never wanted to coach football. And trust me, no one *else* has ever wanted me to coach football either.)

Here's how it went down with my friend and financial planner, Andy Young. We first connected on LinkedIn, and soon we began occasionally meeting for lunch. One day, through the natural course of conversation, Andy said, "Hey James, I'd love to bring you and your wife in to take a look at your financial plan. Doesn't cost anything, I just want to take a look for you, if that's helpful."

I didn't slam the door in Andy's face. In fact, I was thankful. I wanted an expert financial planner to take a look at my finances. Plus, by this point, Andy was a friend, and I *wanted* him to get more business. I wanted him to win. If I could help him by becoming his client—and get top-rate financial planning services in the process—then it was a win for both of us.

So, my wife and I accepted his offer and met him at the

office. Andy walked us through the framework his firm used with their customers, but in a way that spoke specifically to our needs and goals. It was easy for Andy to tailor his presentation because he already knew so much about me. He knew I owned my own business, he knew my wife and I were building a house, and he knew we were interested in growing our family—because he had spent time investing in our relationship. It was obvious he understood our particular scenario and that he genuinely cared about our success. Trusting him with our money became an easy choice, and we ultimately became his client.

> If you've built the relationship in a genuine way, and if what you're offering is genuinely valuable to the other person, it's simply a matter of a friend helping a friend.

Content-Based Networking works the same way. If you've built the relationship in a genuine way, and if what you're offering is genuinely valuable to the other person, it's simply a matter of a friend helping a friend.

Now, I don't have a magic compass to give you that tells you when it's the perfect time to leverage your relationship and tell someone more about who you are and what you do. What I can tell you, however, is that after implementing Content-Based Networking and helping over a hundred other people use it effectively in a variety of different industries, I've learned that no one really thinks it's strange. In fact, so far, if you followed the process that's been laid out in this book, you've simply recreated how professional connections are made every single day. Frankly, isn't it even more strange that we will cold email someone we've never met asking for a job or trying to sell them something? Isn't it much less strange to collaborate on mutual interests and then let them know more about yourself?

Also, you don't have to bring it up every time. Many times after doing a collaboration, I *won't* mention that we're a B2B media company that produces podcasts. Because it doesn't feel right. It just doesn't make sense in the moment, the other person's in a hurry, or whatever the case may be. It's not a huge deal—I just ended up with a new friend and a few pieces of content I can share. It's still a win-win. And we can always connect later about the potential of working together.

PRO TIP

While there's no universal rule on the timing of bringing up what you do, here's one piece of advice: Don't make it weird. You're a human being, and you're talking to another human being. It's not strange that you have life goals. It's not strange to offer your services or to let someone know that you're looking for a job.

BUT WHAT HAPPENS IF THEY SAY NO?

Honestly, if you've built a genuine friendship, you'll never get a "heck no." It's never happened to us once, and we've done over 1,000 content collaborations. At worst, your guest will politely decline:

> "I'd love to, but we're already locked into a contract with another vendor."

> "We're not hiring at the moment, but have you checked out Company ABC? They may be a good fit."

> "We're not looking right now, but I know Company X is."

Whatever the response, your guests value their relationship with you, so they usually try to create opportunities for you in other ways.

If you do get a *no*, then don't let it be the end of the relationship. If you were only trying to get something out of this entire process, then I think you missed the point. *The point is the relationship.* Remember? "Life is relationships. The rest is just details." So, invest in your new *relationship*, and let the good things that come from it flow naturally. Longevity in any relationship always wins. It's easy to forget this—and it's where I see a lot of people get stuck—but it's a crucial element of Content-Based Networking. Stay connected. Connect with your new friend on social media. Meet them for dinner when you're in their neck of the woods. Doing something like this just one or two times over the span of a year goes a long way.

And don't forget that circumstances change. A *no* today doesn't mean a *no* forever. Some of our favorite clients didn't begin working with us until years after our first collaboration.

There's never a guarantee that any given guest will want to work with you. However, they'll *never* work with you if you don't step up, let them know what you're all about, and offer to help them out. If you can do that, great opportunities will present themselves to you on a regular basis.

CHAPTER 15

CONTENT-BASED NETWORKING ALWAYS WORKS. (EVEN WHEN IT DOESN'T)

Earlier, I told you that I had started our podcast thinking that CMOs would be our ideal guests. I explained that when I started the podcast, I was interviewing the wrong people in the marketing department.

Well, I lied to you.

Actually, for the first 150 episodes of *B2B Growth,* we were even further off than I told you we were. Before we landed on the right department (which is marketing), we had been targeting the wrong people altogether—we were originally targeting *sales* leaders.

So, for 150 recordings, interviews, and associated content (like graphics and blog posts), we were talking to the entirely wrong group of people. The good news was, we had no problem getting sales leaders on the show. However, when we talked to them about our service, they had zero interest. But here's what they kept telling us: "You know what? Our marketing team may be interested."

Finally, after hearing that enough times, it dawned on us, and we changed directions and started asking marketing leaders to be guests on the show. This pivot wasn't a true failure. We could have literally spent years trying to sell our product the conventional way—by blasting potential customers with dozens of unwanted emails. It would have taken an infinite number of rejections, trial and error, and maybe, if we were lucky, a few people to buy our podcasting service, before we figured out that marketing leaders were the right people. But since we were having conversations with the people we assumed were our buyers, we heard it straight from the horse's mouth that they were not the right people to talk to. If we had just emailed them or cold called them, we would have gotten the same thing as everyone else—a half-polite, "Please stop calling." And then we would have tried harder and harder to sell our product to sales leaders. A rejection would have taught us nothing. But instead, since we had developed relationships, we heard true honesty. Basically, sales leaders liked the idea of what we were doing, but they didn't control the budget for things like podcasting... marketing did.

Plus, at that point we had 150 episodes of a great show, and potentially, 150 relationships who could get us in the door with their marketing counterparts. In addition, we'd saved tons of time and money that most organizations would have spent trying to sell to the wrong people, only to find out after years of effort, they needed to pivot their entire strategy.

This is what I love about Content-Based Networking: It's literally impossible to lose. No matter what, you end up with content and relationships. That's the worst-case scenario. And, the best-case scenario isn't even what you might think: ending up with relationships, creating *content*, and achieving your *goals*. The best-case scenario is actually finding relationships, creating *content*, achieving all your *goals*, and *then* unlocking opportunities you never even knew existed. Sound too good to be true? You don't have to take my word for it. Take Timmy's word.

> The worst-case scenario is that you end up with content and relationships.

TIMMY BAUER: PODCAST HOST AND CHILDREN'S BOOK AUTHOR

Timmy was a phenomenal illustrator and children's book author. But he had a sales problem. His book had a clever story with beautiful illustrations, but still, it wasn't selling. So Timmy came up with a plan. He'd go straight to where children abound—elementary schools. His plan was this: if he could connect with schools, he could set up times where he could read his book—live in the classroom—for kids. After reading, he would hand out order forms for the book, and the awestruck children would go home and rave about the book to their parents. Then their parents would buy the book.

But Timmy's plan gets better.

If he was *really* successful, those parents would buy extra copies—one for the grandparents, one for the cousins, maybe an extra copy for a jealous sibling. Lastly, parents would join his mailing list, follow him on social media, and maybe even become contributors to his Patreon account. Genius.

Next, Timmy thought about *the people* he would need to connect with. He started with the end in mind (get into the school) and realized that he would need to build relationships with schools: specifically, teachers and administrators.

Finally, Timmy was ready for *content*. Timmy decided to start a podcast called *Books for Kids,* where he'd invite those teachers and administrators on his show to talk about the guests' favorite children's books.

It felt like a perfect plan, but there was a problem. The teachers and administrators actually had little interest in coming on his show (honestly, this rarely happens, but in this case, it did). Timmy struggled for a bit with his podcast, and eventually he realized he was overcomplicating things. He didn't actually need to invite teachers onto his podcast to build a relationship with them. It turns out, his value as a children's book author stood by itself. So, he decided to take a more direct approach and just talk with the schools he wanted to visit and offer a free reading if they would agree to let him sell his book afterward. It worked. The sales Timmy generated from his readings were more than enough to sustain the effort. (If you're wondering how Content-Based Networking actually helped Timmy, just hang on, we're getting there.)

After selling his books in schools, Timmy realized that other authors would love to make a full-time income from their children's book. His process was working so well, he decided to package it up and sell it to *other* children's book authors. Timmy had already done all the legwork—building a database of contact information for school administrators, reaching out, following up, scheduling, managing payments, and so on. So Timmy decided to offer a service to his fellow children's authors, where the only thing they would need to do was sign up and let Timmy's team take care of the rest. (He calls it "Performance-Led Publishing." If you're a children's book author, check out his podcast, *Books for Kids*, and connect with him on Instagram by searching @author_timmy.)

Here's where Timmy's Content-Based Networking comes back into the picture—to generate visibility for Performance-Led Publishing and for his service, he resurrected his *Books for Kids* podcast. But instead of bringing teachers and administrators onto the show, he now brings on aspiring children's book authors to talk about topics related to writing and illustrating kids' books. So, he's using Content-Based Networking to connect with the exact people he now needs to build relationships with for his new business, but in a way he never anticipated.

Content-Based Networking didn't work for Timmy right away. He knew it was a valuable approach, but it turns out it was unnecessary for the people he wanted to reach. However, once he built out his platform as an author, he saw another opportunity and was able to leverage Content-Based Networking in a different way.

Again, this is why I love Content-Based Networking. It always pays off, somehow. While I can't predict exactly how Content-Based Networking will work for you, I can give you a couple examples of how it's helped others.

UNEXPECTED SPEAKING ENGAGEMENTS

Timmy's story didn't end with his Performance-Led Publishing business. In fact, while I was writing this book, *another* opportunity popped up for Timmy, and I had to include it. Here's what happened.

Timmy received a phone call that went something like this: "Hey Timmy, this is Tammy. I'm on the Board of Directors for the Arkansas Literacy Association. I was wondering if you'd be available to speak to a few hundred educators during a couple sessions at our 47th annual conference?"

Remember Timmy's *goal*? It was to connect with educators at elementary schools. Now, he's going to be speaking at a conference where he'll literally be giving speeches to several *hundred* educators. And, he won't be pretending to be a "thought leader"—he was literally *invited* to teach educators about topics he truly understands.

How did Timmy get invited to this conference? Well, he wasn't planning on it, but the opportunity bubbled up because he had put himself in the right room with the right people on purpose.

About 18 months before that phone call, Tammy was on Timmy's podcast as a guest. The topic wasn't the "Arkansas Literacy Association," and Timmy hadn't even conjured up the idea of speaking at that conference. But, because he made a purposeful effort to connect with the right people, he was top-of-mind when Tammy needed speakers for the conference.

RECRUITING

Here's another benefit of Content-Based Networking that I've come to expect—it helps you recruit incredible talent that wasn't even on your radar, which is how we found Logan, our Director of Partnerships.

Logan had spent 10 years selling copiers, living a comfortable life and looking for ways to build on his success. He'd been following a company called BombBomb that he wanted to work for. It just so happened that, right around this time, I had interviewed BombBomb's VP of Marketing, Ethan Beute. BombBomb promoted our interview on LinkedIn, where it caught Logan's attention.

Intrigued, Logan began following me and Sweet Fish to see what we were all about. The more he learned about us, the more he liked us. Over the next year and a half, unbeknownst to me, I was a constant voice in his ear by way of the *B2B Growth* podcast.

One day, Logan reached out to me for my advice on a side hustle he had in the works. We connected instantly, and after about five months of back-and-forth, he joined our sales team full-time. I knew Logan was going to be incredible on our team. I figured with him on board, he could double our business within a year or two.

I was way off.

Logan nearly *tripled* our business in six months. No, that isn't some padded or inflated number—straight up, our business increased by over 270% inside of 180 days because of this one hire.

PRO TIP

If you're an entrepreneur reading this, you have to pause a moment and consider the facts: Every company is in constant search of top talent. Finding the right people is a major pain point for growing businesses, hiring managers, and entrepreneurs. Content-Based Networking provides a game plan for finding talented, creative individuals who can take your growing business to the next level.

REFERRALS

I hesitate to write things like, "Content-Based Networking can help you land insanely profitable referrals!" I don't hesitate because I think it's an exaggeration; I hesitate because it's *not* an exaggeration, and I don't want anyone to use Content-Based Networking to just "hack" sales and miss the greatest benefit of the whole process, which is *relationships*. So, as long as you're down with priority one—relationships—then let me tell you about a serious side effect of Content-Based Networking: lucrative referrals. When you use Content-Based Networking correctly, you position yourself for great-fit, often very lucrative, referrals from the individuals you're creating content with.

Take my friend Stephen Mackey. He's the Founder and CEO of 2Words, a character development program specifically designed for athletic directors and coaches.

Stephen started a podcast called *Coach360*, where he invited coaches and athletic directors to come on his show and talk about how they create and develop strong character on their teams. In the first 50 episodes of launching, Stephen struck gold—twice. One, he interviewed dozens of coaches about character development and learned all about the struggles they were facing with their players and how they were dealing with those issues. Secondly, one of Stephen's guests said this after his interview, "Hey, I know someone who was just mentioning they needed a program like this in their schools." (Notice I didn't write "school." I wrote "schools.")

This contact was actually the director for an entire *county* of schools, and they purchased Stephen's program for their entire district, to the tune of about $40,000. Stephen managed to land a deal worth thousands of dollars within just *50 episodes* of his new show, all because of one referral from one guest.

UNSTICKING STUCK DEALS

(This is a true story, we just changed some of the names.)

One of our clients, whom we'll call Endgame Marketing, was about to close a very lucrative deal with a well-known company, which we'll call Stark Enterprises. (Hey, it's my book. I get to come up with the cover-up names). Anyways, the Big Deal between Endgame Marketing and Stark Enterprises stalled—it came to a halt and went nowhere.

Looking to get things back on track, Endgame Marketing decided to invite one of Stark's decision-makers to be a guest on their podcast. (I like to think the decision-maker from Stark Enterprises was named Howard. Is that too far?) The moment the podcast episode with Howard went live, he was so excited that he shared it with everyone on his staff, and the episode began to create a buzz. Then, guess what? Stark Enterprises went back to the negotiating table with our customer, Endgame Marketing. The deal was moving again.

(Don't worry, I used real names for this next story.)

Another one of our customers, Eric Sharp, CEO at ProtoFuse, also used Content-Based Networking to unstick a deal. He'd gotten an inbound lead from a certain company that matched his ideal customer profile. So Eric presented them with exactly how ProtoFuse could serve them. They thanked him for his proposal, but then things went dark.

For a while, Eric wrote it off as just one of those opportunities that didn't work out. However, around the same time, Eric began working with us at Sweet Fish to produce a podcast. Figuring he had nothing to lose, he invited the president of the company onto the podcast for an interview.

Eric never brought up his stalled proposal, but toward the end of the interview, the president of the company said, "I know you sent us your proposal a while ago. Honestly, ProtoFuse was the second-highest quote we received, but still, we'd love to work with you. Is there a way we can try out a portion of your services to get our team comfortable with you guys?"

Eric, of course, was more than happy to oblige.

If Eric hadn't used Content-Based Networking to continue his relationship with the president of the company, Eric wouldn't have learned their real issue—price. And, without that information, the deal would have fallen through the cracks. By reengaging the president of the company through an interview for the podcast, Eric was able to learn more about their business, their needs, and how he could help them.

YOU MAY GET TO MEET YOUR HERO

If you haven't figured it out by now, I have a man crush on GaryVee. I'm obsessed. But even with that obsession, I never made it my company's mission to interview him, because, well, he isn't our ideal customer. And, as I've said before, Big Name Influencers don't really help you expand the reach of your content.

So far, I've focused on the *goals*, the *people*, and the *content* that maps to our success. But sometimes when you press towards the destination, you find some treasures along the way.

Here's another story of a benefit that came directly as a result of Content-Based Networking:

I was sitting in a small office in Chattanooga, Tennessee. There was nothing especially remarkable about the space—a garage-style door to my left, some desks to my right, and a couple of stools in the center of the room. I was straddling one of those stools trying not to look nervous.

This next interview wasn't going to be good. It wasn't even going to be *great*. It was going to be one of those moments I'd remember forever.

In he walked.

GaryVee.

That's right. It wasn't the focus of my life, I hadn't hinged my success on it. But, by using Content-Based Networking, I actually met the one influencer I'd been following my entire entrepreneurial journey. I met my superhero.

And I didn't just get to meet him. I *interviewed* him.

So, I began to interview my personal hero, serial entrepreneur Gary Vaynerchuk.

If you're wondering how I was feeling, imagine a 13-year-old girl at a Justin Bieber concert. Then, ramp up the excitement by 1,000%. That was me.

"You ready to get started?" I said to GaryVee, as if this were all totally normal.

Gary nodded.

Sixteen minutes later, the interview was done, and I'd explored all sorts of ideas about B2B sales and marketing with one of the most iconic entrepreneurs of our time.

So, how did I get there, interviewing my personal hero?

It started with another guy, Jeremy. We had collaborated on some content together at one point, and, afterwards, we talked about joining forces to do it again. As we started planning what we'd do, Jeremy wanted to invite a Big-Name Speaker that he had a potential connection with, because he shared offices with a colleague of the Big-Name Speaker.

That Big-Name Speaker was GaryVee.

I don't know if you caught all that, but let me recap:

- First, Jeremy and I did an interview together (Content-Based Networking).
- Next, Jeremy and I decided to collaborate on another content series (Content-Based Networking).
- Lastly, Jeremy had a connection that allowed me to spend 16 glorious minutes with my entrepreneurial hero.

So that's the story of how I finally got to meet, the one and only, GaryVee.

And it all started with Content-Based Networking.

* * *

To wrap up, here's the one thing I hope you take away: With Content-Based Networking, there's really no way to lose. It's all upside. You'll definitely end up with new relationships and great content. You'll likely also end up accomplishing your *goals*. And, by putting yourself in the right place with the right people, you'll be prepared to seize opportunities you didn't even know existed.

CHAPTER 16

COMMON PITFALLS (AND HOW TO AVOID THEM)

Isn't it nice when someone who's been there and done that gives you a simple trick that will save you tons of time?

"Hey, that new restaurant doesn't take credit cards."

"Apple Maps takes you to the front of the building—but you actually want to park in the back."

"Seriously, don't bother watching that movie. All the best parts are in the trailer."

This entire chapter is designed to save you a ton of time and frustration. After helping lots of customers make Content-Based Networking a pillar of their business, and after helping to create thousands of pieces of content, we've seen some things. Lots of things.

There's no need to make the same mistakes we've made—or that we've seen others make. Here are a few of the most common traps people often fall into when they are first starting out with Content-Based Networking (and how to avoid them).

1. TARGETING INFLUENCERS

If there's one thing you want to avoid in Content-Based Networking, it's this mistake. And, unfortunately, it's one that almost everyone makes if they haven't been warned.

Don't target influencers.

Wait...what? Isn't that *exactly* who you want to feature in your content? Nope. Here's what people *think* is going to happen when they try to land a Big-Name Influencer on their show:

> "If I can just land Miss Influencer on our show, everyone will listen to it."

Here's the problem with that concept: First of all, especially when your content is new, it's going to be very difficult to land Miss Influencer on your show. She's probably not even going to reply to you. But, even if you *do* get her to say yes, guess what? She has *no reason* to share your content. Think about it—just since last Monday, Miss Influencer has been on 20 podcasts, she was featured on 40 videos, 200 people blogged about her, and the Instagram picture of her morning salad has 9,200 comments. Unless your last name is Spielberg, she's not going to mention she was on your show. Here's the great news: The *exact* opposite is true with practitioners and decision-makers. You get the opposite experience with an expert who is *not* an influencer.

When you ask Miss Expert Who's Not an Influencer to be on your show or blog, you'll likely get a "Heck yes!" I have thousands of yesses to prove it.

But it gets better.

Think about the friends of Miss Expert Who's Not an Influencer. Who are they? They are the *other* people you want to connect with. Basically, when you interview one expert on your show, someone who can help you reach your *goals*, you are gaining access to their entire network. And it gets even better. They aren't just letting you get to know their network, they're basically shining *their* spotlight on you, the way you've shined yours on them. When they share your show with everyone in their network, they're essentially saying, "Hey, check out this person. They're awesome, and so is their content."

This spotlight effect is now going both ways, compounding with every new piece of content. My advice is this: Don't ruin it by chasing influencers.

2. FOCUSING ON DOWNLOADS

In Content-Based Networking, views and downloads aren't a primary goal. In fact, they're really not a goal at all. This is super important that we get this right. I can't tell you how many people get so caught up in increasing their downloads or views that they miss the boat right in front of them. The audience size, downloads, views, reads, listens, whatever, aren't even secondary. They're super tertiary. (Yeah. That's supposedly a real word.) Honestly, I don't care how many downloads my content gets. I didn't at the beginning, when no one had heard of our company, and I don't care much now that our podcasts are getting over 100,000 downloads a month. In fact, we grew so rapidly by *not* focusing on downloads. We focused on our guests and on creating solid relationships, so when our guests finish their interview, they feel like rock stars. Those relationships with our guests are where our business opportunities come from. Focus on those relationships and don't fall into the "How many downloads can we get?" trap.

3. THINKING YOU NEED AN AUDIENCE TO START

Far too many people let the fear of a zero-person audience hold them back. I could explain this logically (everyone has to start at zero at some point), or I could just go into how everything plays out.

Honestly, audience size rarely comes up in conversation. It's pretty simple to say, "Hey, I'm starting a podcast on rescuing animals, and I'd love to hear your thoughts, based on your experience as the manager at an animal shelter." It's not weird that you don't have an audience. And frankly, it never gets weird. "Hey, I'm halfway through a photography series where I've been taking pictures of the best restaurants around town. Do you mind if I show up to take some pictures?" No one complains about free advertising. They just don't.

4. ROMANTICIZING THE CONTENT

Far too many people get romantic about the content, or the audience they are trying to build. I can't say this enough: *Content-Based Networking is primarily about the relationship with the guest,* and secondly, it's about the audience and the content.

Yes, at some level, the quality of the content matters. But don't sacrifice your relationship with your guests, at all, for the content or the audience.

> **PRO TIP**
>
> Here's a quick rule of thumb to understand the impor-
> tance of your guest relationship versus your audience
> and the content:
>
> - In the **short run**, all of the rewards are going to come
>   from the relationships with your guests.
> - In the **long run**, you'll see rewards from your content
>   and your audience size.

5. MAKING IT ALL ABOUT YOU

OK, hopefully I've done a good enough job pushing the relationship more than the content itself, but I still need to point this out:

Don't fall into the trap of thinking the content is all about you.

Sure, you probably know by now not to make your content collaboration one big sales pitch about your product or service.

But here's another way people make their content all about them: they think about what they're interested in instead of what is interesting to the people they're trying to build relationships with.

Don't be that person. It's not effective, and it's just not a good look.

6. CREATING PIE IN THE SKY CONTENT

OK, so here's a content-related mistake people make. Yes, I know I went on and on about how the content isn't the most important thing. It isn't. But, there's no reason not to make your content as good as possible without messing up goal number one: creating relationships. In fact, the better your content, the more future guests will want to be on your show. So at least eliminate major content mishaps, like this one:

> *Don't make your content all pie in the sky. Instead, center it on specific action.*

If you've been reading this book, you've noticed I've harped a lot on making your content *actionable.* Here are a few ways to do that:

- Use real-life examples as much as possible in your content, and feel free to ask your guest, "Can you give me an example of what you mean?"
- Be specific. If the conversation/content sounds super vague, then toss in some numbers and specificity.
- Sometimes, you can frame your content in some form of list (i.e., "3 Ways to Nail Your Audition"). When you format your content into a list, it helps your audience follow, and it also helps your guest keep their thoughts on a straight line.

OK, I think I've made the point strong enough:

Create action-oriented content.

* * *

While I gave you some mistakes to avoid, I believe, incessantly, in this truth: Be ruthlessly married to doing something, to taking action, to just starting, whether or not you have it all figured out. I gave you a few major roadblocks to avoid, but the biggest roadblock is always fear or overanalysis. Don't let fear stop you, and don't think too hard about it. Just dive in.

CHAPTER 17

STOP HOPING AND MAKE IT HAPPEN

I know I don't know you very well. And I'm not sure exactly what your dreams are. But my guess is, you have dreams. And they're really big.

Maybe you're hoping to reform education as a congressperson. If that's the case, I have some news for you: I don't know exactly how to get you there. And if you're trying to train dolphins, I'd have to pass you off to my wife. Or, if your goal is to sell software to construction companies, I don't know much about that either. But you know what? Someone *does*.

Someone is out there, waiting for a congressperson to reform education. Someone is out there hoping to hire the world's hardest-working dolphin trainer. And someone else is out there who needs technology to help make their job at the construction company just a little easier. Someone is out there, waiting for *you*. Maybe they're crossing *their* fingers, hoping they bump into you. Maybe they've been betting on the same serendipity that you have. They're probably out there, just hoping they find you as much as you're wanting to find them. But here's my question: Should we all really leave life-altering relationships like that up to chance? Are hope and serendipity our only options when it comes to creating relationships that could lead to our dreams coming true?

I'm not buying it.

I personally don't believe the only options are chance, luck, serendipity, or hope. I just can't believe in leaving something as big as our goals and dreams up to chance encounters. And, while I know serendipity and hope are incredibly inspiring, I don't want *you* to spend your life just hoping you'll bump into the right people. I think we can all strive for something far more. Something purposeful. Something intentional. We all know that we need relationships to see our dreams come to life. It's like we're standing at the front door of our dreams, fumbling for the key. We know that something powerful is on the other side, we just somehow can't find the key that unlocks the door.

I hope this book can be *your* key. I hope that after reading this, you feel equipped and empowered to create the exact relationships you need to achieve your goals and dreams.

I'm not exactly sure how you came across this book. But if it was simply serendipitous, I hope it's the last time you had to wait for serendipity to intervene. My hope for you is that after reading or listening to this book, you'll be able to define your dreams, then create genuine relationships with the exact people that can help you turn those dreams into reality.

Don't just *hope* you find those people. Make it happen.

TEXT ME

This entire book is about building genuine relationships. And the relationships that have had the biggest impact on my life are with people that make themselves available. So if you ever want to chat with someone about your goals and dreams, other ideas from this book, or Taylor Swift's latest album, send me a text message at 407-490-3328. I'd love to hear from you.

ACKNOWLEDGMENTS

JESUS

I became a Christian when I was 15 years old at a summer camp in southern Oklahoma. When Christ captured my heart in the summer of 2001, I started my lifelong pursuit to love God and love people.

I believe that I'll spend eternity in Heaven, but not because of anything I can do myself. My belief isn't rooted in my good works or my attempt to live a good life. I'm a firm believer that you can't earn your way to Heaven. Instead, I believe that my eternity is secured because of the faith I have that what Jesus did on a cross over 2,000 years ago fully paid for my sins. Christ's death redeemed my soul, allowing me to spend eternity with a perfect and holy God.

If you're interested in stepping into a relationship with Jesus, I would love to be a resource for you. Text me anytime at 407-490-3328.

LISA

To say that I out-kicked my coverage is the understatement of the century.

When I married Lisa, I married a woman who puts other people ahead of herself every single day of her life.

She's the most thoughtful, empathetic, joyful, patient, graceful, and caring human I've ever met. She's brilliant, articulate, and a fantastic communicator. She's hands down the greatest thinker and the best problem solver I know. Her heart breaks when others are hurting, and she does everything in her power to make the hearts of others hurt a little less.

It's insanely hard to start and grow a company. But I'm convinced it's even harder to be married to someone that's trying to do it. Lisa has been there for every high and every low of the roller coaster called entrepreneurship. She's been unwavering in her support throughout every financial scare and emotional breakdown. I can say with confidence that our business would not be where it is today without Lisa's endless support.

The fact that I somehow convinced her to marry me is beyond my comprehension. I hit the jackpot.

Lisa—I love you more than words can possibly describe.

PAUL FAIR

Plain and simple, this book doesn't exist without the outlandish amount of work that Paul poured into it.

He took a bunch of ideas, combined those ideas with stories from our customers, friends, and our business...then masterfully blended those things together to write the words you see in this book.

Paul—When I think about the impact I want to make on the world, this book is a big part of it. And this book would have never seen the light of day without you. You've spent years honing the craft of creative storytelling, and I am beyond grateful that you generously applied your hard-earned skill to this project. I could say "thank you" a million times, and it still wouldn't be enough.

KENNY ORTIZ AND JEFF KAYLOR

I can't write a book about relationships and not thank two of the best men that I know.

Jeff is a masterful creator of unforgettable moments, is outlandishly creative, and has an endless optimism like nothing I've ever seen before.

Kenny is a brilliant thinker, a wealth of knowledge, and I've never met someone with more passion for the grace and hope that Jesus gives us.

Jeff and Kenny challenge me to love better and think bigger. My approach to faith, relationships, and business have been deeply shaped by their influence on my life.

Jeff and Kenny—I'm a better man because of you. Thank you so much for your friendship.

TIMMY BAUER AND STEPHEN MACKEY

Building a business from the ground up is really freaking hard. But it's a little bit easier when you're doing it alongside guys like Timmy and Mackey.

The businesses that these two are building are impacting the next generation in such a powerful way, and I'm incredibly grateful to have a front row seat on their quest to make the world better.

Timmy and Mackey—Your faith, your encouragement,

and your perseverance inspire me more than you know.
Thank you.

MOM AND GRANDMA

It's easy to believe you can accomplish great things when
you've been raised by two women that are ruthlessly supportive of everything you've ever done.

Mom and Grandma—I wouldn't be the man I am today
apart from the foundation you gave me. I love both of
you so much.

LOGAN LYLES, BILL REED, RYAN DRAWDY, AND LILY MELNYK

I suck at most things. So I'm incredibly grateful to be surrounded by the four incredibly smart humans that make
up our leadership team at Sweet Fish.

On top of being brilliant, each of them embodies our
core values: Love people well. Never stop learning. Own
the result.

There's no way our business would be where it is today
apart from them.

THE ENTIRE SWEET FISH TEAM

At Sweet Fish, we're on a mission to educate 1 million leaders every single day. Because when leaders learn, the world gets better.

A mission like that never becomes reality without a team of incredibly skilled individuals that are dedicated to seeing it come to life.

Getting to do meaningful work with people you love and admire is a dream. This team makes that dream real for me.

BRANDON REED, MAC SOUTH, AVEN PITTS

Every year we pile into an RV, van, or airplane and set sail for our annual BroTrip. It's an action packed three to four days of belly laughs, flatulence, and adventures that we'll remember for the rest of our lives.

I don't see these guys as often as I'd like, but when I do, we pick things up like we saw each other yesterday. It's comfortable. It's real. And they make me laugh so hard that I may or may not pee myself a little.

They know my rough edges like the backs of their hands, and they love me anyway. My life is so much better because these guys are in it. Thanks, fellas.

BLAKE BOZARTH, LUCAS MCCURDY, DALE DUPREE, PATRICK HODGDON, ERIC WILLIAMS, CHARLIE MCKENZIE, AND ERIC SHARP

I love hanging out with people, and I love talking about business.

The men listed above allow me to smash those two things together every single time we meet up. When I'm with any of them, my heart comes alive. I walk away from our conversations with a renewed passion and energy for the entrepreneurial journey.

They inspire me. They teach me. They fill me up. Thank you.

DON AND DONNA GREEN

When it comes to in-laws, I struck gold. They have welcomed me into their family with so much warmth, and I am beyond grateful for them.

On top of being generous, supportive, and ruthless at the card table...their parenting skills are second to none. It must've been tough figuring out how to raise a child to become the greatest woman of all time...but they did it! ;)

RYAN EBER AND MATT MANCINELLI

For my first couple years in Orlando, I was attached at the hip to these two...and I'm better today because of it.

From Matt, I learned what radical generosity, intentionality, and strategic thinking look like.

From Ryan, I learned how to make someone feel like they're the only one in the world that matters in that moment.

Thank you both for your friendship and your influence.

THE CREATORS OF RED VINES LICORICE AND THE GENIUS THAT DEVELOPED CHERRY COKE ZERO

I love you.

SANGRAM VAJRE, ETHAN BEUTE, JOHN ROUGEAUX, SHARON TOEREK, STU HEINECKE, ERIC OLSEN, SAMANTHA STONE, AND CHAD SANDERSON

There are few things more fulfilling in business than having customers that turn into friends.

To each of you—Thanks for your friendship and for

the trust you put in our team. I appreciate it more than you know.

JEFF FLOURNOY

Jeff took a chance on me when I was 24 years old, giving me an opportunity to make a real impact in his business.

Jeff showed me what it took to be an entrepreneur, and it's hard to believe that Sweet Fish would exist apart from Jeff's presence in my life.

Jeff—When you asked me to move to Orlando, you changed the trajectory of my entire life. Meeting Lisa and pursuing entrepreneurship have been life altering experiences for me...and they happened because of the chance you took on me. There's a reason this book is dedicated to you.

ABOUT THE AUTHOR

JAMES CARBARY'S podcast, *B2B Growth*, has been downloaded over 3 million times and is a top-ranked podcast according to *Forbes*. James has interviewed world-class thought leaders, such as Gary Vaynerchuk and Simon Sinek, and has been a contributor to *Huffington Post, Entrepreneur*, and *Business Insider*. When he isn't writing a book or running his business, Sweet Fish Media, you can find him sipping Cherry Coke Zero, eating Red Vines licorice, and trying to figure out how he somehow convinced the most incredible woman on the planet to marry him.

Made in the USA
Coppell, TX
21 October 2021

64423900R00114